"*Maximizing Your Sm* ... n
our lives—dwelling w ... t
and soul into our hom ... or large,
this book will inspire you to rethink every inch of your dwelling to create space and live peaceably with your belongings. Kathryn's book is one of my new favorites to recommend to my organizing clientele who are committed to simplifying their lives. Kathryn will inspire you to embark on a delightful journey to create small space living. Live well where you dwell!"

Marcia Ramsland, The Organizing Pro (www.Organizing Pro.com) and author of *Simplify Your Life*, *Simplify Your Time*, and *Simplify Your Space*

"*Maximizing Your Small Space* is a great example of my own home mantra: 'It's not what you don't have, it's what you do with what you have.' Kathryn provides oodles of useful and affordable home organizing and decorating tips, information, and resources. She also shows through her personal stories of hospitality that a home doesn't have to be large in size to be graciously grand in spirit."

Kitty Bartholomew, former HGTV host of *Kitty Bartholomew: You're Home*; decorating correspondent for ABC-TV's *The Home Show*; and author of *Kitty Bartholomew's Decorating Style*

"Kathryn's heartfelt book about real-life small space homes is packed with practical and stylish tips, ideas, and resources to help you take your home from drab to dazzling, no matter what size your space or budget. She wisely dispels the notion that small space living is restrictive and instead artfully teaches us that organized small spaces enable us to enjoy life more."

Laura Leist, CPO and founder of Eliminate Chaos, author, and past president of the National Association of Professional Organizers

"Kathryn's tips and resources for organizing and decorating small kitchens and dining areas will enable anyone to dine beautifully at home, whatever the size of their space. And Kathryn is indeed correct that one can artfully entertain in a small space. Her clever and affordable real-life entertaining ideas and tips will bring ease and joy in sharing one's small home with others."

Olga Krasnoff, author of *Dining by Design*, media spokesperson, lecturer, former Macy's senior interior designer, and event planner for Tiffany & Co.

"If you want to maximize your baby's small nursery space while simultaneously improving the health of your child, Kathryn's book *Maximizing Your Small Space* offers simple solutions. You'll discover how to easily green your baby's nursery and transform it into a nontoxic, organized, and serene space."

Lisa Beres, founder of Green Nest and www.RonandLisa.com, national media spokesperson, and author of *Just Green It!*

Maximizing Your Small Space

Maximizing Your Small Space

A ROOM-BY-ROOM GUIDE

KATHRYN BECHEN

SPIRE

© 2012 by Kathryn Bechen

Published by Revell
a division of Baker Publishing Group
PO Box 6287, Grand Rapids, MI 49516-6287
www.revellbooks.com

Spire edition published 2022
ISBN 978-0-8007-4118-1
eISBN 978-1-4934-3591-3

Previously published in 2012 under the title *Small Space Organizing*

Printed in the United States of America

The stories and examples in this book are based on real-life individuals and situa-
tions the author has experienced. Specific details, names, and identifying character-
istics have been altered, left out, or turned into composites to illustrate a point yet
honor personal privacy. Any resemblance to a specific person or situation a reader
may know is purely coincidental. Also, though the author's writing style is that of
a supportive coach cheering her readers on to take action, the information, ideas,
and tips contained in this work may not be suitable for every person, situation, or
reader, and the author is not engaged here in this work in rendering actual consulting
or professional advice or services. In addition, just because the author mentions
an organization, individual, resource, or website in this work, even as one of her
personal "favorites," it does not mean that the author necessarily professionally
endorses the individual, website, resource, or organization or their products or
services. Readers should also be aware that internet websites, resources, and books
listed or mentioned in this work may have changed or disappeared between the
time this book was written and when it was purchased or read.

Baker Publishing Group publications use paper produced from sustainable forestry
practices and post-consumer waste whenever possible.

22   23   24   25   26   27   28   7   6   5   4   3   2   1

For my football-player-sized hubby, Steve,
who's artfully shared several small home spaces
with me during thirty-plus years of marriage.
With love and gratitude to you,
my dear sweet man.
And
in loving memory of our beloved
Scottish Fold kitties,
Beau and Monique,
who were my devoted writing companions
and lovingly knew how to "dwell well"
with us in several small space homes
for fifteen years.

Contents

Acknowledgments

Birthing a book is a long process, and I feel truly blessed and honored that there have been so many friends, teachers, mentors, clients, and acquaintances over the years who have in some way large or small, tangibly or intangibly, inspired and encouraged my career as a published author. Although I'm not able to name each of you here individually, I thank all of you collectively, with my sincerest affection and heartfelt gratitude.

Special thanks to:

Steve Bechen, my hubby and biz partner extraordinaire. Huge thanks, *babe*, for keeping my computer tech and accounting stuff up to date so I could focus on writing this book. And love, hugs, and kisses for all your moral support. How in the world did I come to marry a *steadfast/numbers/ techie/handyman guy* who knows just how to patiently and unconditionally love this *organized/high-spirited/creative word lady*?

Without my publisher, this book would still be a concept in my head and just a few notes on my computer. So with profound gratitude I thank the Revell team at Baker Publishing Group for believing in me as a first-time book author. Special thanks to senior acquisitions editor Chad Allen, who listened with interest to my original book proposal and forwarded it to my wonderfully enthusiastic executive editor, Vicki Crumpton. Huge thanks, Vicki, for all the efficient steps you immediately took on my behalf to make this book come to pass and for your expertise in the editing process. Also a special thank-you to Janelle Mahlmann, assistant marketing manager, for coordinating the marketing and PR efforts for this book. Your vivaciousness and enthusiasm as one of my main go-to people are very much appreciated.

I believe in the grace of God, and ultimately I thank the Lord Jesus Christ, my true God, from whom all my life blessings flow, for planting the gift of writing in my spirit. Lord of my life, thank you for the opportunity to touch other people's lives through words. *I hope I have made you proud.*

Letter to My Readers

Dear Readers,

Small space dweller, I understand you because I'm one of you. Whether you live in a city, a small town, or the country-side—in an apartment, condo, dorm room, or perhaps a cute little house you fondly refer to as a "cottage"—I've lived there too, so I know the challenges and frustrations, as well as the glorious freedoms and blessings, of living in a small space.

Economic times have changed drastically both in America and across the world in recent years. *Builder* magazine's 2010 "Home for a New Economy" was designed at just 1,700 square feet. And according to the *Wall Street Journal* in 2009, for the first time in twenty-seven years, home buyers opted for smaller homes. *CNN Money* reports 7 percent smaller—or one average-sized room. We're rethinking whether or not we really *want* a huge home, a big yard, and all the "stuff" that goes with that lifestyle. Do you?

I can comfortably say, *I don't.* You see, I can admire beauti-fully designed and decorated "McMansions" with the best of them. I have toured and written about them, organized them for clients, and had close friends and colleagues who live in them. But I also know, from hearing the comments of homeowners who dwell in large houses, that the cost—economically, personally, and professionally—of paying for, cleaning, and maintaining a big home can be phenomenally restrictive rather than life-enhancing, at least for some people. *Restrictive and stressful is not how a home should feel.* On the contrary.

In addition, many people today feel strongly about the "green living" movement and are committed to leaving a positive legacy for future generations, including not using up more than their fair share of our planet's precious resources. Small space living is one step in that direction because it conserves consumption of land and energy, and it also uses fewer material goods and furnishings than one would purchase to fill a larger home space.

Perhaps your own small space living journey has been, like mine, somewhat of an evolutionary process. My husband, Steve, and I have personally chosen, over time, to continually live in small spaces for a variety of reasons. Admittedly, it didn't start out as a conscious choice. When we were mere twenty-one- and twenty-three-year-old newlywed babes with stars in our eyes, we chose to rent a tiny yet adorable house ($20' \times 20'$) purely for economic reasons. We had college loans to repay and new furnishings to buy, and we knew we would not be living in that town indefinitely, so we opted for the cutest place we could find for the cheapest rent.

At the time, like most ambitious, red-blooded Americans, I had the mindset that a small home meant a lack of living well. I longed for a beautiful large home and yard one day, and we were willing to work long and hard for it. Over time though, after multiple career relocations, it became apparent that for us buying and maintaining a large house was just not practically feasible for a variety of reasons. And so began my quest to adjust my "house size mindset." I searched extensively for creative and practical ways not just to live but to *dwell well* in a small space.

In 1992, long before most people had even heard of a "professional organizer" or there was a HGTV cable channel, I started my own business, *Organized With Ease*, and became a hands-on office organizer, seminar leader, speaker, and consultant. My business was featured often in our local media. I worked with many clients who owned large homes and offices and were drowning in massive amounts of disorganized stuff. Closets bulged. Garages groaned. Piles of papers proliferated. And yes, my clients sometimes cried, *and even divorced*, because of it.

As I spent hour after hour of intense work sorting and organizing, I listened to their stories. That clinched it for me once again that small space living was the path I wanted to personally continue on so that I felt free to have meaningful life experiences and rich relationships, rather than be weighed down by maintaining the material stuff of life. I realized that small space living was a viable and attractive lifestyle *choice.* And my husband agreed.

It also dawned on me over time as I was adjusting my house size mindset, that it wasn't the huge amounts of space in large custom homes that I was drawn to—it was their fine aesthetic details. Bingo! Once I had that beauty epiphany, it released me to create a practical *and* aesthetically pleasing *small home.* That fact combined with the quality time I shared with others there, and I learned to happily dwell well.

I've lived in thirteen small home spaces of every size and shape all across the U.S. over the past thirty years, and now I'm pleased to share with you in *Maximizing Your Small Space* what I know and practice in my own life. In the pages of this book, we'll journey together—like having a good friend and coach by your side—as we explore the nooks and crannies of all types of small homes and rooms. Then you can get *yours* in just the right amount of order so that you and your family don't feel it is claustrophobic, but instead *perfectly petite.*

I hope you'll come to think of *Maximizing Your Small Space* as your lifelong "small space bible" that you can reliably refer to time and again as you progress through the stages of your life, moving from one home to another. I encourage you to read it through all in one sitting and then go back and refer to specific chapters as you need them. And (unlike your ol' eighth-grade English teacher!) I hope you'll write in the margins and highlight favorite tips and passages that motivate, encourage, and inspire you along your journey. Take notes on whatever ideas will help you get organized. Get out your colored markers and have fun. *Whatever it takes!*

So come on, *let's get started!*

Kathryn Bechen
San Diego, CA

"Small spaces give us the opportunity to live sincerely, forcing us to choose which of our possessions make our hearts sing."

Kathryn Bechen

1

Maximum Living in Minimum Space

Which small home dweller are you?

- You've just turned eighteen and are now footloose and fancy-free from Mom and Dad. You're headed off to college across the country where you'll share a miniscule dorm room with a roommate you've never met.
- You're a young single working person, living out your jet-set fantasy life in a tiny studio apartment in a trendy and expensive area of New York, Tokyo, Paris, or some other fascinating city.
- You're a newlywed couple who's just bought your first little home and are very proud of it.
- You're in a midlife career transition due to a company downsizing, and you've landed in a new city and state. Housing costs are much higher than your

former city, so you've had to squeeze your large family into a much smaller home.

- You've just retired and are selling your large family home to buy a condo in a warmer climate.
- You're an elderly widow or widower who has just moved into a pint-sized assisted living space.

It really doesn't matter what your small space circumstance is or how you came to live in your particular small home. What really matters, I firmly believe, is that you (and your family, if you have one) know how to *dwell well* there.

Can that really be achieved? Absolutely, because small space living isn't just about the space; it's a *lifestyle choice* that's rich with blessings and—*if you make it so*—with beauty.

Big House Blues versus Small Space Grace

Consider these real-life stories:

I recall a close friend whose husband built not just one but two large homes. He had them beautifully decorated with the finest furnishings that money could buy. I remember her story many years later with a tinge of sadness, because with increasing frustration she complained to me that she couldn't go out for a fun day of antiquing with friends, or even to a coffee shop or movie, because she always had to be at home coordinating and overseeing the gardener, the maid, and the pool man, or waiting for a handyman or delivery truck. Her executive husband expected nothing less than perfection at home at all times, and he wanted her to be there at his demanding beck and call.

One day when she was at my own home, this monetarily wealthy woman said with tears in her eyes, "I love coming to your cozy and charming home because it feels warm and welcoming. It feels like a *home*. I feel like I'm rambling around in a huge, cold *museum*; my house may be beautiful, but *it has no heart.*"

Contrast her story with another friend of mine. A gal of very modest financial means, she rented a 500-square-foot apartment yet served Steve and me a delicious lunch at her kitchen card table and folding chairs. A lovely tablecloth, her grandmother's floral dishes, and a vase of fresh flowers graced the table. We held hands and prayed over her festive meal and thanked God for our blessings. Laughter and conversation flowed and wonderful aromas came from her oven. That night we slept snugly in her little living room on her sleeper sofa which was covered with a quilt lovingly handmade by her favorite aunt. Hers was *the blessing* of a small space home: cozy hospitality, fond memories, caring. She indeed knew how to *dwell well*.

Still other friends of ours rented a nice but teeny tiny apartment that had beautiful furniture and was spic-and-span. With a baby on the way, they sectioned off a nursery area in their own bedroom and hung a sweet, colorful mobile over a fresh white crib. When a group of us gathered for a meeting in their little living room, ice-cold tea and laughter flowed. None of us complained a bit about feeling cramped—we simply enjoyed our time together.

When we were newly married, another couple who became good friends owned a picturesque little home situated on the edge of a beautiful canyon, surrounded by gorgeous trees. Many a night we enjoyed grilled hamburgers and hot dogs on their patio, where we admired the glorious sunset and had great conversations.

Another dear friend invited me to her lovely small, one-bedroom high-rise apartment overlooking a beautiful lake. It was cozily and cheerfully decorated with rustic pine furniture and a pretty floral chintz sofa where we sat sipping tea while she showed me photos of her family. What a lovely way to get acquainted with someone who became a good friend I've now known for twenty-five years.

Since my humble newlywed days long ago, I've attended many beautiful dinners and lavish events because of my writing career and my husband's commercial real estate banking career, and I've enjoyed them. Yet I can say with conviction that these happy memories of time shared with authentic friends in their small homes are etched fondly in my mind *forever*, while the details from many of the big fancy dinners have long been forgotten.

How to Dwell Well

If you wonder whether you're maximizing not only the *living space* of your small abode but also *the life* you're living there, here are some things to consider on your own small space journey:

- Attitude is everything! You see your small home as a blessing and a beautiful escape from the expense and rigors of big home living and maintenance, rather than as lack of any kind.

- When you enter your front door after a long hard day, you immediately feel (and maybe even say aloud), "Ah, I'm *home*."
- You can easily find what you need when you need it, because your home is organized effectively in a way that suits *your* lifestyle.
- Your paperwork and filing is up-to-date and is not strewn all over the dining room table.
- Your bathroom functions as a soothing, spa-like environment where you revive and rejuvenate from the stressors of life, no matter how small the room is physically.
- You can easily cook meals that are both nutritious and attractive and can clean up your little kitchen with ease.
- You understand that renting is fine and that it's not necessary to own your place unless you choose to do so.
- You have a home office space that is comfortable and functional so you can conduct your personal and business affairs efficiently.
- Your garage, if you have one, houses your cars instead of acting as an overflowing storage unit.
- Your yard, if you have one, is easy and cost-effective to maintain because all your lawn maintenance tools are organized and in good repair.
- Your sleeping area(s) are serene and orderly, ensuring you a good night's rest.

- Your storage needs are taken care of in a manner that works for your lifestyle and budget.
- If you like to read, you have a little library organized in a way that makes finding your books easy.
- You have an organized space to enjoy one or more relaxing hobbies.
- If you have kids, they have an orderly and comfortable place to do their homework.
- You can have guests over to your home and feel comfortable entertaining them without feeling cramped.
- You don't put off having guests to your home until you get a bigger place; you enjoy them *now.*
- Your kids do not have to contact you by intercom or cell phone from another area of your home because it's so large.
- You and your mate share a special bond because you have time to enjoy wonderful life experiences together since you are not tied to endless big house maintenance, chores, and yard work.
- If you live in an urban area, you enjoy ease of transportation, partake in exciting cultural and sporting activities, and frequent beautiful green parks.
- You've put your unique personal stamp on your home by decorating it with items that you've collected and that speak to your heart.
- And last but not least, you feel *proud,* and not at all *apologetic,* about your little home because it's a comfortable and welcoming place for you, your family, and your guests.

Getting Started with Order

The most important ingredient of every small space that dwells well is *order*. Yes, uh-huh—good old-fashioned organization, plain and simple. You simply cannot live well in a small home without a foundation of order. That doesn't mean your home will always look picture perfect. But to function for you efficiently and effectively and to be a pleasant place to come home to, a foundation of order is paramount.

So let's begin the organizing process by asking yourself a few questions about your own current little abode so that you can go from where you are to where you ultimately want to be. Write your answers and notes right after the questions if you're so inclined.

Questions to Assess Your Small Space Needs

1. When you walk in your front door, how do you want to *feel*? What's the ambience you'd like to come home to? How does it feel *now*?

2. Which room do you spend the most time in? Is that the room you *want* to be spending the most time in?

3. Do you have sufficient natural lighting from windows, or does it feel too dark?

4. How many people live in your home? Will any be moving in or out in the future?

5. Are there any particular areas of your home that really annoy you? If so, what are your plans for change?

6. On a scale of one to ten, how organized do you feel your space is currently?

7. Are you happy with every single room in your home?

8. Is it easy to have guests come to visit for dinner, and stay overnight if necessary? Do you think they feel welcome and not cramped, or like they are imposing? Do you feel comfortable hosting overnight guests? (Some people don't.)

9. Are you happy with your current storage systems?

10. Are you comfortable with your paperwork systems?

11. Do you have a home office space or do you long for one?

12. If you have indoor hobbies, do you have a space set aside for them?

13. Does your home accommodate any special health needs you have?

14. Is your bedroom/sleeping area conducive to a good night's rest?

15. Can you cook and clean up easily?

16. Does your bathroom organization enable you to get yourself ready easily?

17. Is your laundry space organized enough so you can do your laundry efficiently?

18. Are your car(s) housed sufficiently, and is there adequate space for making repairs?

Keep these questions in mind about your own small space so that you can implement my ideas, tips, and resources as we make our way together through this book.

Please Note: *Always keep personal safety a priority as you work through the principles, ideas, and exercises mentioned here.*

——————— YOUR SMALL SPACE NOTES ———————

2

Downsizing
for Rightsized Living

Before we get down to the nitty-gritty how-to of organizing your possessions and rooms in order to dwell well in your small home space, let's backtrack a bit and assume for a minute that you aren't living there quite yet. Instead, you or perhaps an elderly loved one have just started considering the big "D" word—*downsizing*—which may strike fear, angst, and dread in your heart.

Why? Because I'm guessing that you or your dear one have amassed many years' worth of stuff in and around your big home, three-car garage, storage shed(s), and yard. Not to mention that you've played out a lifetime of family memories here and you're feeling . . . um . . . *overwhelmed*, and maybe a little sad, about the whole prospect of downsizing, even if you *are* excited about it too.

Or maybe you're in the same situation as one of my former clients. She was the recipient of a huge marital home because of a divorce, but was left with a few sticks of mismatched leftover furniture, and boxes and more boxes of disorganized stuff to sort through and move. Overwhelmed and sad were her middle names at that point. Fortunately we succeeded in sorting out the boxes and downsizing her into—you guessed it—a small home she bought and decorated to her heart's content with fine French antiques, which suited her new life perfectly!

Never fear, feeling overwhelmed is normal! And here's some good news: you *will* get past it and will soon have a wonderful new "rightsized" home and life. Also take comfort in the fact that you're not alone; as I wrote this a Google search for "downsizing your home" turned up 424,000 results.

List Love and Binder Bliss

I'm a list lover, pure and simple, because lists not only help us remember things, they also help clarify our lives and our plans as we write thoughts down. If you're at the stage where you're even *thinking* of downsizing, I recommend you buy a 3" three-ring binder and some clear page protectors where you can physically collect all your thoughts and ideas as well as keep any paperwork and literature you gather along the way, all in one organized and convenient place. I've done this for every move I've ever made, and it works every time! You can buy the binder and page protectors at any office supply store.

Case in point: A friend of mine recently shared with me that her elderly parents spoke to her about possibly selling their large rural home and moving into a city condo, apartment, or retirement center. So she took them to tour properties one weekend, just to take a look. As we talked about the process they went through, she told me that in hindsight she would have suggested her parents make a list from the outset, clarifying their needs and wants on paper before they started their tour. As the old saying goes, "Let your fingers do the walking" to save time, energy, and angst. Having a binder along when they toured properties would have given them a convenient place to take notes and to store all the literature they gathered.

Physical and Emotional

Be prepared as you go through the experience of downsizing your home that it's not just a physical process. It's also an emotional time of letting go of possessions and sometimes of sad memories, and also a time of remembering happy, meaningful family moments that took place there.

It takes careful thought, time, and many decisions in order to move artfully into your new life stage. My friend's dad, for example, repeatedly mentioned to her that they would not have room for their china cabinet in a small condo dining room, which was true. I suggested to her that perhaps what her father *really* wasn't ready to let go of was the idea that their china cabinet symbolized so many dear memories of them all gathered around the table as a family. Once she realized that, she assured him that they'd still have happy family times together in the new space.

It's normal to go through an array of emotions during your downsizing process, and it helps to get through it by keeping your mind's eye focused on the end result of a lovely new rightsized home, decorated in a style you love, in a neighborhood that's just right for you at this new stage of your life.

Destination Dreaming

Once you've bought a binder, have fun with the downsizing process! Pour your favorite hot or cold drink, cozy up by the fireplace with your binder and your favorite pen, and put on some relaxing music. Close your eyes, dream of what your future space and life will look like, and take notes.

Perhaps you're envisioning a cute-as-a-button, charming condo in a quaint little town or a cozy cottage in the woods. Maybe your dream home is a sleek, modern, urban apartment with all white and chrome furniture, an elevator, and a doorman. There's no right or wrong at this stage; for now you're simply dreaming, which will eventually get you to the final stage of a practical plan.

If you have a mate and/or children, you should all do this dreaming exercise and compare notes. Compromise will likely be in order, and with written notes you can cross things off your list and add new ones until you're all happy.

Possession Obsession

Start "editing" your current possessions before you ever put your home on the market; if you're a renter, start about eight weeks before your move. Don't get caught in the trap of "We had no idea our house would sell in a week!" mode, or you'll end up stashing endless boxes of stuff into a moving van and paying twice as much as you need to move things you don't even want anymore.

One thing to consider before you even start the process of sorting your possessions is the idea of selling your existing home furnished. Of course, you'll still have to go through and decide which personal items to take to your new place, but if you don't mind parting with your current furnishings, or if you prefer to get new ones, selling your home furnished is a viable option.

Here's a plan to reduce the stress of possession editing. With a floor plan of your new, smaller home space in hand, start with the rooms in your current home that you use least often. Take your binder and pen and walk through every room, including outer areas like the garage, storage sheds, and yard. Take notes for each room and evaluate your belongings carefully, from largest to smallest. Here's where you're going to decide what to take with you, what to give away to charity or family, what to sell, and what to toss in the dumpster. (Yes, I know for some of you, that feels like another dirty "D" word. But trust me on this, you're gonna grow to *love* this dumpster dumping thing!)

Family Love

It's wise to consider involving the whole family in the sorting and tossing process. "Many hands make the work light," as the old saying goes. Possessions have differing sentimental value and meaning to different family members, so it helps if all family members are present, or are at least available by phone for some of the decisions.

Case in point: I recall my elderly friend who was downsizing and selling her home of many years to move far across the globe. She was sure her fifty-something son still wanted his maple desk from elementary school that was housed in her den. He lived in a small, chic, modern urban apartment across the country. Possessing a totally different design sense than his mother, the son had no interest in the desk. However, he could say nothing to convince her otherwise. Lesson here? The item you may donate to charity if you edit possessions by yourself may be the very item your grown child wants to keep as a family heirloom. But then again, *maybe not.* Ask, and honor their wishes.

It's also okay to ask adult children and other family members to come and pick up the things they want, and it's wise to tell them a firm date for removing the items from your home. Also be sure that every family member gets something special, which sometimes involves *kindly* negotiation.

Let's Get Physical

Once you have a written plan in your binder, it's time to get started on the physical work. Keep in mind that it's best to plan to sort items for periods of no more than two hours at a time. You'll feel less overwhelmed and will make better decisions if you take regular breaks and allow yourself time to digest what you're doing.

Here's how to sort and sift:

- Gather some large drawstring trash bags, various size boxes with lids, marker pens, masking tape, and some large white adhesive-backed labels. Sort items into boxes/bags labeled Toss, Donate, Give to John, and so forth. Make arrangements to remove the containers from the house as soon as possible to keep the process rolling. (And no fair bringing anything back into the house, "just in case." Remember, I *know* some of you!)

- As you go through each room, ask yourself, *Do I want, need, or love this?* This is the time to decide if you really want all your books, children's toys, DVDs, CDs, tools, artwork, and that big huge bread maker in your kitchen that you haven't used in ten years.

- Sort through your clothing closets and get rid of items you no longer wear. Be realistic, and *please* don't be like one of my organizing clients who told me the story about how his mother, although he was now twenty-three years old, still had his little baby sleeper hanging in her hallway closet, complete with spit-up stains on the front, "for when he had kids." (Needless to say, he and his beautiful new bride weren't interested!)

- Remember now: sort, toss, donate, sort (kind of like lather, rinse, repeat when shampooing your hair!). Don't assume you can take everything from a larger home with you and just cram it in if you want a new smaller space that's *pleasant* to live in once you get there. Make wise choices and keep only what you need and love.

Okay, now that you've got the hang of how to edit your possessions before your move, let's take a little walking tour through each specific room.

Fabulous Foyer

Look at your existing entry or foyer and compare it with your new smaller one, if you even have one. Will your big antique hall tree and ninety-eight-pair shoe caddy really fit in your new foyer? Open the coat closet door and ask yourself whether you really need that fur coat from Aunt Matilda if you'll be spending winters in balmy Florida from now on. And what about the spare key caddy on the closet shelf with keys that no longer fit any lock you own? And those extra light bulbs? Will they fit the fixtures in your new space? Get rid of things like this, and you have my permission to be *ruthless*!

Kitchen Kudos

Sorting and editing a kitchen takes more time than nearly any room in your home, so allow double time for this room. Not only are there many small dishes and items to sort and pack, but as the hub of the home, kitchens are laden with memories, sometimes making it harder to decide what to keep and what to toss. Take extra time to reminisce with family members as you sort through items and tell stories about the happy times around your kitchen table. Also consider when moving to a smaller kitchen that you may not have a pantry for things like canned goods and large cereal boxes, and your cupboards may not go all the way to the ceiling. Refrigerators and freezers are usually smaller too, so plan accordingly.

Family Room Fun

Perhaps you once had large family gatherings for holidays, or all your teenagers' friends came over for big pizza parties in your family room. Those days are no more and you may have elected not to have a family room in your new smaller abode. This is the time to sort through games, trophies, wall memorabilia, and the like, and give them to children and grandchildren, or to charity.

Living Room Love

Your huge sectional sofa and big-screen TV may not fit well, or look good either, in your new smaller living room. Consider getting rid of those and see chapter 6 for new furniture ideas.

Master Boudoir

Ah, the master bedroom, where we love and live! Your new smaller bedroom may not accommodate a king-sized bed and two nightstands along one wall, so be sure to take wall measurements before you move and to notice if there's a closet door to take into account. You may want to consider a smaller bed.

Bedrooms and Guest Rooms

Chances are, if you're moving to a smaller space you will have fewer bedrooms, or maybe none at all if it's a studio. Also keep in mind, one bedroom in your new home may have to serve as a room for kids returning from college for the summer, as a guest room, and as a home office all in one, so get rid of anything that says "dated bedroom."

Bathroom Bliss

Small bathrooms notoriously lack storage, so you'll want to be sure to get rid of any old extra raggedy towels, to toss lotions and potions you never use, and to ditch any old magazines you read while soaking in the tub.

Den Diva and Library Love

If you're a "den diva" and have cozy cases of books and knickknacks galore, be sure to carefully weed through these. You may not even have a den or library in your new smaller digs, or that room may have to double as your hobby room. Keep only the items and books that are truly dear to your heart.

Hobby Haven

Yes, hobbies can be accommodated in small spaces, which I will teach you about in chapter 14. 'Til then, evaluate whether you really need one thousand sticker packs for your scrapbook collection or four hundred colors of thread for your counted cross-stitch hobby. Get rid of anything that you won't be working on in your new space—perhaps your quilting hobby has simply done its time.

Basement Blahs

Ah yes, the beautiful basement—often home to anything that hasn't found a place elsewhere. Now's the time to go through your old teaching supplies from when you taught third grade thirty years ago, or to donate that old hamster cage your four-year-old (who's now thirty-four) once took delight in showing to his friends. Remember, you're likely to *not* have a basement at all in a smaller home, so *toss, toss, toss*!

Home Office Heaven

If you've had a whole room dedicated to office space in your current home, that's a luxury you probably won't have in your smaller space. But with laptop computers and a decorative folding screen, you can easily set up a corner or convert a closet into a cozy home office. Try to make your current home office as paperless as possible before moving. That way you won't have to pay to move and store large file folder boxes off-site if there's not room for them in your smaller home. Check with Goodwill Industries or other organizations in your town to see if they accept boxes of documents for shredding like they do in my city. And in some cities, local businesses or TV stations sponsor shredder events.

Laundry Room Lowdown

Go through your laundry area and get rid of any socks that have fallen behind the dryer, crusted dryer sheet containers, and old detergent boxes with just a tad of detergent left in the bottom. In your new smaller space, you may have fewer shelves to store laundry supplies. So please say bye-bye to any items you no longer need *before* you move.

Garage/Storage Shed/Yard

Moving to a smaller home space with perhaps a one-car garage or no garage, or to a condo or apartment building with underground parking that has no regular garage like a home does, poses a challenge for some downsizers. The best way to evaluate your garage and storage shed possessions is by considering your new lifestyle. Will you still be mowing the lawn? If you're going to be living in an urban high-rise apartment home like I do, trust me, you'll no longer need a garden hose or lawn ornaments. Will you have a handyman on call 24/7 so you only need to keep a hammer, a few nails, and a drill? Do you still need that big snow blower you used on the East Coast if you're moving to Hawaii where you'll be making sandcastles on the beach instead of chubby snowmen in your yard?

Again, ask yourself as you walk through these spaces: "Will I really *use* this item in my new lifestyle?" If not, surely there is someone you know who'd be glad to take it off your hands. In the unlikely event that you might need something you do get rid of, it will likely be cheaper to buy a new one at that time rather than pay to move and store your older model anyway.

Collection Obsession

What's your particular "collection obsession"? Okay, I admit it. Organized soul that I am, I once owned enough teapots to rival Imelda Marcos's shoe collection! And Steve still has about fifty Santa Claus figurines he's collected since we were in our twenties. (We both love them, so we have no intention of parting with them.)

When you downsize, you'll want to make some decisions about your collection(s), and I hope what I am about to tell you about my teapot collection will help you decide.

I enjoyed everything to do with collecting my teapots . . . at one time in my life. But after I moved across the country and then packed and unpacked and dusted and arranged them during several local moves, I decided my teapot days were *over.* So I lovingly wrapped most of them up and donated them to my favorite thrift store, where the proceeds went to a charity dear to my husband's heart: animal shelters. The glass curio cabinet that had housed them for fifteen years, had been expensive to repeatedly move, and was a Herculean task to dust, I paid to have hauled to a consignment shop. My cabinet sold quickly and some other collector is now enjoying it—*and dusting it*—instead of me. And I'm a happy gal with no regrets!

Give serious consideration as to whether *your* particular collection(s) will still bring you joy once you move to smaller quarters, or whether your greater pleasure would be to give it to someone else who would enjoy it more at their stage of life.

Going Green

As you work through the downsizing and rightsizing process, please remember to dump as little as humanly possible into our landfills. Instead, recycle by donating your items to those who can use them, be they family, friends, or charity.

Celebration Time

Okay, now that you've gone through every room in your current home, taken notes in your binder, and donated, sold, or given away things you no longer want or need, it's time to celebrate. You've accomplished a big task! Treat yourself to dinner out or to a movie. As you contemplate moving into your new smaller digs, be thinking of creating your first lovely dinner gathering with new friends and neighbors.

—————— YOUR SMALL SPACE NOTES ——————

3

One-Room Wonder

*How to Live Happily and Practically
in Just One Room*

If you've ever lived in just one room, you know what a small space challenge it can be. Yet time after time I've overheard people excitedly describe how free and happy they feel living in a studio apartment or condo, or how they long for the "good old days" of dorm living when everything they owned fit nicely in just one room.

Years ago when I was contemplating my move to Southern California, I looked at possible small space properties with a realtor. I can still vividly recall touring the cutest one-room condo overlooking the beautiful Pacific Ocean. The building was an elegant white stucco with black scrollwork Juliet balconies and fancy urns at the front entrance. It was so adorably charming that my heart longed for such a sweet little space where, free from the everyday cares of house maintenance, I would have time to write, walk to the neighborhood village for a cappuccino, and savor the oh-so-blue ocean beyond. I didn't buy that particular little coastal abode, but I did find a wonderful small rental that I loved for all the same reasons. So whether you're living in the studio apartment of your dreams, a less-than-darling dorm room, or have just moved into a tiny assisted living space, you *can* make it an organized and pleasant place to live!

Let's get started!

Function Junction

First and foremost, if you are considering a one-room living space, remember that *all living functions* must take place in that one room (except the bathroom, of course!). Storage is pretty much nonexistent. That means you're going to have to get creative, since you're going to cook and dine, sleep, entertain, enjoy hobbies, study, dress, and maybe work and do laundry all in one small room. If ever it was time to get organized, it's *now*!

Easy Entryway

Entering your home after a long hard day should make your heart sing, no matter how small the space. For that reason, start by hanging a lovely wreath on your front door to welcome you home. Choose a color and style that coordinates with your interior colors and décor.

Faux Foyer

Chances are you won't have even a smidgen of a foyer and instead you'll walk right into your room the minute you open the front door. You can easily create a "faux foyer" feeling by placing a small bedroom nightstand along the wall near your front entrance. Nightstands are handy since they have drawers where you can deposit your keys and coins upon entering, thus avoiding clutter. I even found a basket that holds our shoes and is just the right size to put underneath my own foyer nightstand, which helps to avoid a messy looking entrance. Another small basket on top holds outgoing mail and errand items.

Mirror, Mirror

Hanging a mirror above your foyer nightstand expands the space visually and allows for a quick checkup on your appearance before going out to work each day, so that both you *and* your home look tidy.

Coatrack

Place a standing coatrack in the corner near your front door to hold your coats and umbrella. From brass to wood, there are many styles available. Some even have a special base designed to hold umbrellas. As an alternative to a standing coatrack, mount decorative hooks on the back of your entrance door to save floor space.

Kitchen Kudos

To get started organizing your little kitchen, remember to *KISS: Keep It Super Simple!*

Dish Delight

Consider white all-purpose dishes and clear glassware that you can use both for everyday and for entertaining guests. They'll look fresh and uncluttered if you have open shelving, and you can complement them with colorful cloth napkins that can be stored in a wicker basket on your counter.

Sparkly Glasses

It's easy and attractive to mount under-the-counter holders to hang stemmed glasses, saving precious space in your cabinets. My husband and I found some clear acrylic holders at www.ContainerStore.com. Install some twinkly tubular lighting under the cabinets to add a sparkly glow to your glasses.

What's Cookin'?

Think about how you eat *every day*. Will you really be cooking *and* baking? Or do you tend to prefer a carton of yogurt with a few apple slices and some cheese and crackers? When you have a hankering for a warm meal, do you microwave a frozen dinner, roast one chicken breast in your mini slow cooker, or dine out? Stock your kitchen supplies accordingly and be selective about buying space-eating appliances and gadgets. Why buy an electric can opener when a small handheld one will do?

Utensil Heaven

Buy one favorite set of attractive, nested cookware, a butcher block of sharp knives, a nice set of silverware, spatulas, wooden spoons and other cooking utensils, a slow cooker, and a few plastic storage containers for leftovers. Again, don't buy more utensils, cookware, and containers than you need.

Clear Containers

If you have open shelving in your kitchen, round clear glass or heavy acrylic containers with lids work well to hold things like sugar, coffee, tea bags, cookies, crackers, rice, and so forth. Canning jars with lids are another inexpensive alternative.

Sparkling Clean

Use a portable plastic cleaning caddy with a handle to store your cleaning supplies under your kitchen sink. You can carry it to the bathroom to clean, avoiding duplicate storage of cleaning supplies.

Drawer Dilemma Solved

If you have few drawers in your kitchen like I do, think outside the box. I bought a beautiful antique silver urn to hold all my wooden and other cooking utensils upright, and I put it right next to my stove. You might also have some wall space next to your stove to hang a few cooking utensils on decorative hooks. Next to my kitchen sink I have a small crock with a pretty scene painted on it that holds my pot scrubby and vegetable brush. A decorative metal basket on my counter houses placemats and napkins. And a basket on top of my fridge stores my paper plates. Look around for containers you might already have that you can repurpose.

Basket Bonanza

Baskets are bliss when it comes to the kitchen. Store folded cloth napkins and placemats in them on your counter or on top of your fridge. Pretty napkin patterns and colors make for a lovely little bit of art, and different basket weave textures add a cozy ambience to a tiny kitchen.

Tray Time

Trays work great for entertaining in a small space, and they work well if you prefer to dine on your sofa instead of at the kitchen table. I buy colorful stacking melamine trays with artful scenes. When they're not in use I stand them upright against my counter backsplash in lieu of a painting. They wipe off easily too.

Trash Tidbit

Buy an under-the-sink rolling trash can unit so you can easily pull your trash can in and out. It'll be hidden from sight and will save floor space.

Going Green

Put a small extra trash can for recyclables in the cabinet under your kitchen sink.

Dish Drainer Diddy

If you have double sinks, store the dish drainer rack right in the sink to save counter space. Mine fits perfectly in a standard-size sink.

Towel Tip

A decorative hook on the wall or inside the cabinet door under the sink works well for hanging your dish towel.

Fun Fridge

If your refrigerator is the under-the-counter kind, remember to buy food package sizes accordingly. A large watermelon and gallon-size milk probably won't fit. And forget more than one or two magnets on the front; too many will look cluttered in a one-room home.

Savvy Cookware Storage

The lower stove drawer, if you have one, is a good place to store pans and bakeware. Mounting a pot rack behind the stove or suspending it from the ceiling will save space and artfully display attractive cookware. You can also store pots and pans right in the oven, but be sure to remove them before turning the oven on.

Spice-a-licious

Install spice holders inside your cabinets or on the backs of the doors, or use hard plastic turntables to store spices and canned goods.

Lovely Living Room

The living room in your little one-room abode will likely have to do multiple duty as your living room, guest room, hobby room, TV room, study space, and maybe even home office, so function and furniture layout are important, as are a few other factors.

Neutral Upholstery

To achieve a serene and clutter-free look, I suggest solid neutral upholstery for all your furnishings. Also keep knick-knacks to a bare minimum and instead opt for large colorful wall art, which will visually expand the space.

Loveseat Love

A loveseat-size sleeper sofa works great in a small space living room. You can sleep on it, or if you have a regular bed, it can serve as a guest "suite." Place end tables on each side of it with nice lamps on them for reading. A clear glass coffee table in front of it will make the room look bigger. An arm-less loveseat or futon is even better as it gives the illusion of more space. Trunks also work great as coffee tables and do double duty, storing things like extra blankets, photo albums, and memorabilia.

Furniture Placement

When placing furniture in a one-room space, less is more. Think *function first*. Either place all the furniture artfully around the perimeter of the room so there's a large space in the middle, or create mini-zones (e.g., one zone for sleeping, one for dining, one for TV/reading, and one for your desk/home office).

Sweet Slumber

Consider a twin bed, or if more than one person is living in the space, go for a trundle bed, which stores underneath the twin bed and can be pulled out. The beauty of a twin or trundle bed is that during the day it can double as your sofa if it has some nice big pillows against the wall for seating comfort.

Loft Bed

Another sleeping option is to "loft" your twin bed near the ceiling and use a ladder to get up to it. You'll need a handyman who can help you build it so it's safe. By lofting the bed you'll have room underneath to create a cozy little living room complete with a couple of small arm chairs or a sofa and coffee table. Or put a desk and filing crates under there to create your home office and/or hobby area. Lofting is a good use of space as it does double duty.

Murphy Bed

We all know about the quintessential Murphy bed that stores in the wall and can be pulled down. The blessing is that during the day you'll have lots of room. The bane is that when the bed is up in the wall it can look like there is an empty hole in your living room and you may have to move furniture around. You also might not be strong enough to hoist a bed up and down into the wall, no matter how clever the lever.

Nifty Nightstands

Instead of using a heavy nightstand and lamp next to your bed, stack three large wicker baskets. Or try a tall round wicker hamper with a lid that can easily be moved if you are pulling out a trundle bed. Use a lightweight lamp.

The baskets can serve as storage for bedding, towels, and clothes. Keep items on top of the baskets to a minimum to avoid clutter.

Bathroom Brigade

Chances are if you live in a one-room home, your bathroom is the size of a postage stamp. The secret here to storing all the things you need is to get rid of anything you don't use and to go vertical up the wall.

Vertical Vivaciousness

Buy a cabinet with doors that stands over the back of the toilet. I have one that I use to store extra shampoo and conditioner, manicure supplies, tissues, and extra razors. On the opposite wall is a matching cabinet where I store towels, and underneath that cabinet hangs a rod so that my bath towel is handy right when I get out of the shower. That's a lot of storage in one tight little 3′ × 5′ space!

More Nifty Nightstands

A bedroom nightstand with drawers works great in a tiny bathroom. You can store manicure supplies, razors, and so forth in the small drawer, put towels on the shelf under the drawer, and put a basket on the floor under it for toilet paper or rolled up hand towels.

Shoe Caddy Storage

Hanging over-the-door clear plastic shoe caddies works great in the bathroom, too. Since the pockets are clear, you can easily see at a glance what's in them. They can hold items such as razors, over-the-counter medicines, extra shampoo bottles, soaps, and rolled-up washcloths. And remember, if you hang it over the shower rod, be sure to hang it on the outside of the shower curtain.

Pedestal Sink

If you're lucky enough to have one of those gorgeous pedestal sinks, the unlucky part is the lack of counter space for personal care items when you're grooming. One solution is to place a narrow bookcase or cupboard with doors on either side of the sink. The tops will function like a counter while you're getting ready in the morning, and you can use the shelves below for storage.

Drawer Divider Diva

If you're not one already, turn yourself into a drawer divider diva! Buy plastic divided silverware trays to store small items such as your toothbrush, razors, and dental floss. You can also buy rectangular clear plastic lidded craft boxes with square divider compartments for storing hair barrettes and the like. I bought mine at Michaels.

Laundry Area

If you're really lucky, you'll have a washer and dryer in your one-room space. If not, stackable units can be adapted to fit the size of a standard closet. I had a stackable washer/dryer in one apartment we lived in, and I loved it because I didn't have to bend over to get my clothes out of the dryer. Add a shelf above the unit to store your laundry supplies, or store them in a nearby cabinet.

Home Office Suite Office

Can you really work from home if you live in a one-room home? Yes! These days it's a breeze with laptop computers, scanners, and compact all-in-one fax/copier/printers. The key element will be setting up your workspace efficiently. Just like in the bathroom, remember to go vertical up the wall for extra room. Also, I encourage you to consider any hobbies that can be integrated into this work area and plan accordingly for storage.

Desk Darling

There are a myriad of desk styles and designs available. When choosing your desk put function first, then choose the decorative style you like best. Consider a desk that has at least one center drawer for office supplies and three drawers on the sides, two of which will hold letter-size files. Another cost-effective desk option is to cover a cut-to-fit board with your favorite fabric or wallpaper and place it on top of two two-drawer filing cabinets.

Place your desk in a corner or against a wall so you can post a bulletin board in front of it to hang notes and reminders in an organized manner. If you arrange your desk in a corner with a two-drawer filing cabinet on either side, the tops of the filing cabinets will also give you more workspace to spread out papers.

Be sure your desk has a comfy chair. One option is to buy an office chair from an office supply store and make or buy a slipcover to match the other upholstery so it coordinates with your décor. That way you can move it around as needed and use it for more than just an office chair. I did this and I *love* my slipcover!

"Office-in-a-Box" Armoires

Another type of desk you might consider is the amazing office-in-a-box armoire. It looks like a fine wooden cabinet, with two doors that swing open to reveal shelves, cubbies, drawers, and a space for your computer. Some units even include foldable chairs that store inside when not in use.

Put wicker baskets on top of your armoire for storing things such as paper, or put your printer up there. My husband has used an office armoire for twelve years now and loves it. I helped a client of mine choose one to put in her kitchen, and she too really enjoyed working there.

Folding Screen Savvy

If you want to hide your home office in a corner, placing a tall decorative screen in front of the area works great. The screen can also be a decorative statement if it has a lovely scene painted on the front. Screens work great as camouflage in small spaces; I have a white weathered wood folding screen in my own home that looks like old shutters and hides my air purifier. Another white metal folding screen stands on my high-rise terrace to hide my air conditioner.

Office Supply Solutions

Since you're living in a small space and have created an "office corner," you'll want to keep your paperwork to a minimum if you can. It's best to keep as many documents as possible on your computer, preferably a laptop to save desk space so that you can be as portable as possible. A word of caution though: be sure to follow a data backup plan and also keep your really important paper documents in a fire-proof box.

If you don't have a desk with filing drawer space, buy portable plastic filing cubes from an office supply store. Get the ones with lids so you can stack them and move them around easily. You'll also want a cube right by your desk to hold hanging files to keep track of your daily paperwork, or what I call your WIP (work in progress) files. This includes active papers such as invitations, items you've ordered, and any daily life papers that you are currently acting upon.

Cozy Closet Storage

Chances are you have only one large closet in your one-room home. This needs to do multiple duty for your clothes, linens, luggage, and broom. The key here is to use every inch of space well, way up to the ceiling. If your closet has a regular swinging door, use the back of that too.

It's worth purchasing a closet organizing system like Elfa from www.Elfa.com so you can make it fit the closet exactly. The store's staff will gladly help you customize it. Ikea.com also has closet organizers. Be sure to plan to double-hang rods and figure out how many shelves you'll need before purchasing.

Skinny "velvet" hangers are great for small space closets because they don't take up much room. Store sweaters and folded shirts on the shelves. If you have a small chest of drawers, you can place that right in the closet, or buy plastic drawers that stack to hold your socks and underwear.

Clear plastic bins with lids can go on the top shelf or on the floor to store your winter clothes, sheets, and blankets. Clear lidded plastic shoe boxes work great for women's shoes. If your closet has a regular door instead of a sliding door, use an over-the-door shoe holder. The bigger the pockets, the better they fit men's shoes.

If you have no other alternative than to store your mop and broom in your one closet with your clothes, buy wall-mount hangers and mount them on one end of the wall. Store the vacuum next to them, leaving some space next to your clothes.

Style File

Remember as you are organizing your little one-room home to give it your unique decorative stamp. It's nice to frame personal artwork, or you can enlarge your colorful digital photos onto canvases to create interesting and personalized décor. And that lovely vase, pitcher, or basket you bought while on vacation? Use those containers for storage as well as to artfully personalize your space. I heard about a ninety-four-year-old lady who hired an interior designer to decorate her assisted living space. That goes to show that no matter how small the space and whatever your age, having pleasant surroundings that exude your personal style is a wise way to *dwell well!*

One Last Tip

My last one-room home tip for you is that mirrors work great to visually expand a room. Placing one on the wall opposite your sliding glass patio doors or opposite a window will reflect light and appear to open up the space. Or buy 12″ × 12″ mirror tiles that stick right on the wall and mirror a whole wall that way. If you're renting, be sure to ask your landlord's permission before you try this.

One-Room Living Resources

Closet Organizing Systems
www.ContainerStore.com
www.Elfa.com
www.Ikea.com

Coatracks
www.CoatRacks.com
www.CoatRackShack.com
www.Target.com

Desks, Office Armoires, Filing Cabinets, Folding Screens
www.EthanAllen.com
www.HomeDecorators.com
www.OfficeDepot.com

Hard Plastic Turntables
www.Target.com
www.WalMart.com

Home Organizing Supplies
www.ContainerStore.com
www.OrganizedAtoZ.com
www.ShopGetOrganized.com

Office Chair Slipcovers and Reupholstery Services
www.CozyCottageSlipcovers.com
  (Owner Teresa Bennett made my office chair slipcover and I love it!)

"Office-in-a-Box" Armoires
www.BallardDesigns.com
www.PotteryBarn.com
www.Target.com

Office Supplies and Chairs
www.OfficeDepot.com
www.Staples.com

Over-the-Toilet Bathroom Cabinets
www.HomeDecorators.com
www.HomeGoods.com
www.Target.com

Plastic Craft Storage Boxes with Lids
www.Michaels.com
www.Target.com

Plastic Silverware Trays
www.Target.com
www.WalMart.com

Plastic Stacking Drawers
www.ContainerStore.com
www.Target.com
www.WalMart.com

Spice Racks
www.ContainerStore.com
www.ShopGetOrganized.com
www.Target.com

Tubular Lighting
www.HomeDepot.com

Turning Digital Photos into Canvas Art
www.CanvasOnDemand.com
www.Costco.com

Velvet Clothing Hangers
www.OnlySlimlineHangers.com
www.Target.com
www.TJMaxx.com

Wall Mount Hangers for Mops and Brooms
www.ContainerStore.com
www.Target.com

———————— YOUR SMALL SPACE NOTES ————————

_____

_____

_____

_____

_____

_____

_____

_____

_____

_____

_____

_____

_____

_____

_____

_____

_____

_____

_____

_____

4

Small Space Wisdom

Special Small Living Spaces

Certain small living spaces such as high-rises, basement apartments, urban lofts, and RVs have unique space considerations and organizing challenges. I currently live in a mega-story high-rise building in sunny Southern California, where the palm trees sway gently year-round, and I can tell you for certain that my small space organizing considerations, both inside and outside, are vastly different than when I lived in a tiny basement apartment during my college days in the blustery cold Midwest. So as you evaluate your own small space organizing needs, remember to take into account the unique type of space you are living in or are considering moving into, as well as the climate.

Grown-Up Basements

Many homeowners these days are renting out their basements as a way to generate extra income. Others are remodeling their basements for their grown kids or an elderly parent.

With some updated design and organizing strategies, many basements are now very pleasant places to live instead of the dark, cramped, cold basements of long ago. It's all in the details, so take the following factors into account carefully as you are setting up your own space.

The Difference Is in the Details

I fondly recall the adorable basement apartment I lived in with a girlfriend when I was in college. (In contrast to the hideous one my boyfriend lived in with his buddy!) Ours had been remodeled and had a cute little kitchen with lovely oak cabinets and a white tile floor. The rest of the apartment had pale green fluffy carpet and attractive white wooden paneling, all of which made the space cheerful, bright, and inviting, in spite of the tiny windows that let in little natural lighting. Both my roommate and I were ultra-organized, and we pooled our resources to turn our little abode into a cozy study retreat.

Here's what we did, to give you ideas for your own basement space:

- In our tiny living room, two small matching tables served as study desks when we didn't feel like reading on the sofa, and a shelf we assembled housed our TV and kept our college books tidy along one wall.
- We placed our bunk beds up against one wall in our single miniscule bedroom and cozily decorated our beds with handmade quilts and pillows. Each of us had a small dresser on opposite ends of the room for our socks, undies, and casual clothes.

- We shared our one clothes closet, each taking one end. Sweaters and tops were stored in stacked plastic cubes, blouses and pants were hung, and suitcases and extra blankets went on the top shelf. (Suitcases also work well for storing seasonal clothing.)

- We kept our personal bathroom items in plastic caddies on top of our dressers. We carried the caddies with us to the bathroom and then returned them to our respective dressers when we were done so as not to clutter up our tiny bathroom with our individual lotions and potions.

- Because of the small amount of sunlight that came through the tiny windows, we bought green plants that were shade friendly. They added a homey ambience. Silk plants would work equally well.

- We used floor lamps and table lamps for extra lighting, and we also had extra space heaters and a dehumidifier to combat any dampness issues.

- Outside, our cars served as another storage spot. We bought large plastic opaque containers with lids and kept them in the backseat to hold extra household items like groceries and blankets. (Don't use clear containers, which will invite thieves; opaque ones work much better.)

- We chained our bicycles to a rack outside and had a locked, secure storage unit on them for school supplies. Again, use any bit of space you can find for storage, however small.

Special Basement Considerations

You may need to enter your home through a shared entrance, so plan to store shoes and boots inside your own home rather than near the communal entrance. A plastic bin or lidded wicker trunk works great.

Because they're below ground level, basement apartments are darker than upstairs rooms. Often the ceilings are lower too, and even a person of average height can feel cramped. Add extra floor and tabletop lighting, and if you do have a large window, place a mirror on the wall opposite it to reflect light. You can even add a little romantic ambience by stapling strings of tiny white twinkle lights to the ceiling.

If possible, paint the walls and ceiling white or a soft pastel color to create a light and bright welcoming feeling. If you live in a warm climate, a seaside cottage look is nice, complete with pastel blue walls, white quilts, and a wicker rocker. *Ah, basement bliss!*

Buy matching crates or trunks for storage. If you live in a snowy cold climate and prefer a super cozy, dark restaurant look, paint the walls a jewel tone such as deep rust or burgundy and add luxe-style furnishings for a warm, cocoon-like effect.

If you have no garage and/or must park on the street, use your car trunk to store car care items and a safety kit of extra clothes and supplies for inclement weather. Store items in opaque lidded plastic bins.

Again, even if you live in a teeny tiny basement apartment, put a wreath on your front door to welcome you home!

High-Rise for the Space Wise

If you've ever fantasized about living in a high-rise home, I can heartily recommend it because that's where I now live and I *love* it! However, there *are* unique organizing and living considerations to this type of small space dwelling, and high-rise living is not for everyone. Here are some things for you to consider before you rent or buy a high-rise unit:

High-Rise Living Pros

Most high-rises are located in urban areas and, like the one I live in, have restaurants, shops, and other specialty conveniences right outside your front door. From an organizing point of view, that means you don't necessarily need to store a month's worth of groceries or toiletries. If you run out of something you can buy it right away and in smaller quantities. I keep a pretty tote bag right by my front door so that when I need something, I simply walk downstairs and out my complex's main entrance, which is attended by a doorman, and buy my goods just around the street corner.

Also, you may not need to stock your home office quite so fully, as there is often a business center on site. Our building comes complete with several computers and two fax machines. In a pinch, it's nice to know I can likely get online if my own computer goes down, and I really don't need to take up precious space in my home office with my own fax machine.

You also won't likely have to make space in your living room for an elliptical machine or stationary bicycle. Many high-rise buildings have full gyms, complete with every kind of modern exercise equipment you could ever imagine, as well as a swimming pool (or two) and tennis courts.

If you don't feel comfortable entertaining in your small home space, there's often a beautiful large party room you can reserve, or you and your guests can have a barbecue by the pool. And if you're looking to make new friends but don't want to get your small apartment all gussied up for guests, the management often hosts get-togethers, such as breakfasts or "Cider and Cinema" in the building's on-site theater. I've often seen ladies meet in the party room to play bridge.

No need to store a ton of tools either, because with a twenty-four-hour on-site maintenance crew, they'll bring their own hammers and screws. And if you no longer want a garage full of stuff, you'll love the underground parking garages with assigned parking spaces. Be aware, though, that there is usually no place outside your car to store anything. Sometimes you can rent an extra storage unit or crate in the building if available, but those are usually very small.

Since you won't have a lawn, no need to store your yard equipment or drag that garden hose with you when you move in. And you can also say "bye-bye" to your snow blower as snow removal is provided.

The view from high-rise terraces can be stunning, since at least some units view the city lights, mountains, ocean, or a park beyond. However, the terraces are usually tiny with little room for large furniture, and they lack storage space so you'll have to get clever. I have a small wrought iron bistro table and chairs on my terrace that we use for breakfast or a cup of coffee and a chat once in a while. I also placed a decorative metal screen in front of the air conditioning unit to hide it and the things I store behind it.

Going Green

I love the fact that the high-rise building I live in has recently implemented a recycling program. It provides large dumpsters on every floor in our parking garage, so it's easy to take the recycling out while on the way to my car. If you're considering moving into a high-rise, inquire about its "green" program. If there isn't one, ask what plans there are to start one.

High-Rise Living Cons

If seeing your neighbors in the elevator every day isn't your cup of privacy tea, high-rise living isn't for you. With so many people living in such a dense space, you're guaranteed to bump into each other.

Noise can be a problem in some units too, so if you are noise sensitive like I am, be sure to inquire about a corner unit or one on the top floor. That being said, if you also have a fear of heights like I do, you're not going to like the top floor because it will never feel like home if you get nauseated every time you sit on your sofa. (One apartment I looked at on the top floor had a terrace with open railings, and it made my stomach queasy just standing *inside* the sliding glass door!) And if you never use your terrace, that's not a good use of space in a small home either.

High-rise buildings are often built on a campus-like outdoor space in a very compact area. Units are usually compact inside too and are sometimes lacking in light, with windows only on the outside wall. Also, high-rise population density is not comfortable for everyone, so give that serious consideration before moving in if you're selling the family farm or a large suburban home.

As far as organizing the inside of your high-rise home itself, the same organizing principles mentioned elsewhere in this book apply, so happy high-rise living!

Luscious Lofts

Who among us hasn't dreamed of living in a small yet chic urban loft apartment or condo, complete with soaring ceilings, a sleek modern kitchen, stunning city views, and bistros and museums right out our front door?

Or perhaps you'd be happy with a more standard apartment or condo that has a cozy open loft "room" that overlooks your living room and dining areas. An acquaintance of mine uses her apartment loft exclusively for storing her huge wardrobe and dressing table, and she gets ready for work up there every day. The space has a beautiful round window for natural lighting, a spiral staircase, a chaise lounge that opens and stores her jewelry, a special rod mounted on the wall for all of her belts, hooks that hold her necklaces, and a decorative screen that hides her many fashion boots. Talk about a private fantasy land! This type of upstairs loft would also work well as a small library or home office nook, a craft room, or a children's playroom.

The sky is the limit, so tap your imagination to use the space well in a way that works for your lifestyle and family.

Like basements and high-rise buildings, loft living has certain advantages and disadvantages, and you'll want to carefully think about the following before moving in.

Open Sesame

The openness of an industrial or standard urban loft is both a dream and a challenge. It's a dream because of the fluidly open space, but often the only indoor wall leads to the bathroom. All other functions of living must be delineated with items such as furniture, folding screens, bookcase room dividers, or panels of hanging fabric. And storage must be created on your own since it's not built in.

Keep your furnishings simple and the space uncluttered; using large furnishings and art and avoiding small knickknacks works best for creating a streamlined and aesthetically pleasing look. Also, combining sleek modern furnishings and antiques creates a warm, yet sophisticated and chic urban space.

Make a Plan, Stan

The first step when considering loft living is to walk around your prospective space and make a plan on paper. Draw out zones for eating, sleeping, living, dining, and entertaining. Then, and only then, purchase furnishings and organize accordingly if you do choose to live in that space.

Work Around It

Many industrial urban lofts have exposed heating ducts and old brick walls. Work with what you have and place furnishings, art, and storage pieces to complement them. Antique armoires, for instance, work great as storage units or TV centers, look charming next to a brick wall, and add warmth when mixed with more sleek contemporary glass, chrome, or metal furnishings.

Beautiful Bedroom

If your loft has no separate bedroom, you can create one by first placing a large area rug to delineate the space. To create a portable wall and also to provide storage, use tall open book-cases with baskets on the shelves, or buy the style with doors on the shelves. With a long "wall" of bookcases, you can easily store all your clothes, shoes, and books out of sight, and you can use the top for storage by placing baskets up there, too. Or you could place art objects up on top for added aesthetics.

If you're not on a tight budget, a closet organizing company can create a customized freestanding "organizing wall" of shelving for you that will serve as a dividing wall. If you're on a budget, stores like Target have white melamine cabinets that are about four feet tall and have two doors on the front. Place three or four of these side by side for a cost-effective freestanding "wall" of storage. (**Caution:** When creating any kind of freestanding wall of shelves that will stand in the middle of a room, be sure they can be anchored properly to your particular floor for safety.)

Also, since you won't want guests to see a messy bedroom, be sure to position your zones for your other living areas so that your guests don't look directly into your bedroom, and make your bed every day and keep the room tidy. Night-stands with drawers can house your personal essentials to help keep clutter at bay.

Living Room Love

Place your living room furniture to take advantage of your awesome city, ocean, or park views if you have them. An L-shaped sectional sofa without arms works well in an open space. The straight line of its back gives the illusion of a half wall that visually divides up the space, and not having arms creates a space-expanding look. Glass tables and lamps provide an air of sophistication and further expand a small loft. Trunks and ottomans also work well as coffee tables and have the added benefit of storage.

Kitchen Kudos

Freestanding cooking islands provide extra counter and storage space and can either cozy things up or make a small kitchen space feel more chic, depending on whether they are quaint wooden butcher block or sleek metal. Hanging utensils on the wall adds a homey touch, as does hanging a pot rack behind the stove or on the wall next to it.

Glass-front kitchen cabinets add an additional sophisticated flair to a loft kitchen when you display your favorite sparkly glassware. And if your cabinets don't go all the way to the ceiling, place decorative baskets on top of them to store your tablecloths, extra napkins, paper plates, and so forth. Use library steps for access.

Dreamy Dining Room

A rectangular table, with its straight lines, and a rug underneath it will help define the dining space in a loft. An antique buffet can serve as both a storage piece and a countertop if you put a piece of cut-to-fit glass or granite on top of it. It adds a homey ambience to a chic sophisticated space, as does a crystal chandelier. For a more contemporary lighting look, consider pendant lighting.

Art Smart

Since most lofts have soaring ceilings, large tall paintings and nicely framed posters look great on the walls and draw the eye upward. If you have beautiful digital photos you've taken, blow them up onto canvases for unique and personalized art. Beautiful fabric panels suspended from the ceiling can also function both as art and as walls, and depending on the fabric, can be an inexpensive solution. Often pillars are present in lofts. You can faux paint them for a dramatic art effect, and they also help visually separate the space. Additionally, a contemporary arched floor lamp doubles as both lighting and sculpture.

Flourishing Floors

Many urban lofts have concrete or hardwood floors. Large colorful area rugs help to visually divide up the space into living zones and add warmth.

Home Office Haven

Want to enjoy the bright city lights while you type your future famous novel? Place a beautiful desk in front of your soaring living room window and type away! Buy a luscious leather chair, and when you entertain, roll it into the living room for extra seating. Floor-to-ceiling bookcases on either side of the desk and window are stunning and provide ample storage.

Loft Bathroom Living

Chances are the bathroom in your loft is the only room with walls. If your ceilings soar up to a skylight, *hooray!* Take advantage of the natural lighting by placing green plants on top of tall bookcases that go as high up the walls as possible for maximum storage. If you have a pedestal sink, consider putting a skirt around it and storing toilet paper and tissues behind the skirt. Also, the larger the mirror over the sink, the larger your bathroom will appear.

With beautiful city views, soaring windows, artfully placed furnishings, and savvy storage, your loft really can be a luscious small living space!

RV Rendezvous

If you've ever dreamed of driving off into the sunset and never again returning to your home and its constant yard maintenance, perhaps the full-time RV lifestyle is for you. Of course, before you make such a drastic lifestyle change, you'll want to consider whether you feel comfortable leaving your family and current community and downsizing your possessions (if you elect not to keep your stick-built residence while on the road). Also consider whether you and your mate (if you have one) will be able to live harmoniously 24/7 in a tiny RV space that moves . . . most of the time.

If indeed you're all ready and raring to transition to full-time RV living, below are a few organizing tips and lifestyle considerations.

- You'll have very limited space compared to a house, condo, or apartment, so don't take more than you really need. If you do, you'll just be frustrated by too much clutter and too little storage, not to mention increased fuel costs. Remember, you can always buy things along the way if you forget something initially.

- Begin assessing your storage and possession needs by drawing a loose sketch of the inside of your RV so you have a rough estimate of how much space is available, and then plan accordingly as to what things are really necessities to take along. That will, of course, differ for every person, couple, and family, so continually ask yourself how you intend to live on the road. As you load your RV, type an inventory list on your laptop and print it out.

- Use a three-ring binder with clear top-loading page protectors to file your interior RV storage sketch and inventory list and to store other important lists and papers such as campground information. Keep the binder in the front of your RV for easy access while you drive.

- Buy large rectangular lidded plastic storage containers to keep outside when you park your RV. Use them to hold items such as tools, hoses, and extension cords.

- Use smaller rectangular lidded and stackable plastic storage containers inside cabinets to keep like items together and prevent canned goods and bathroom items from rolling around. You can also set up one container with a few office supplies as a mini-office.

- Line your cabinets with nonslip liners to help keep items in place.

- Use repositionable adhesive-backed plastic hooks for hanging things like robes and towels. (Don't poke holes in the wall for hooks as there may be electrical wires behind the wall.)

- Figure out how to make supplies do double duty. For instance, how about using a large cooler as a table-top?
- Use hanging plastic shoe bags to store maps, campground lists, small household tools, and so forth.
- Think vertical and maximize space all the way up to your ceiling. Bathroom towel racks can be hung over the top of a door, for instance.
- Avoid rattling dishes by placing paper plates between regular plates and padding other dishes and pans with dish towels.
- A laptop computer can save space by replacing paper maps, phone books, and reading material, plus it's a great way to stay connected with the rest of the world for news, and with your family and friends via Facebook and Twitter.
- This may be the time to consider an e-reader as your primary "library."
- Remember you will have less personal privacy in an RV so talk this issue through with your family before you hit the road.
- Don't become a campground "clutterbug" and an eyesore to your neighbors by setting up too much stuff outside your RV. Again, evaluate how much you *really* need to take along to be functional and comfortable.

I'm confident that, should you choose to think outside the box and choose a nontraditional small space to live in such as a basement, loft, high-rise, or RV, you'll be able to get organized enough to make it a wonderful experience!

Resources for Special Small Living Spaces

Area Rugs
www.CrateandBarrel.com
www.EthanAllen.com
www.HomeDecorators.com

Armoires and Antique Reproductions
www.EthanAllen.com
www.HomeDecorators.com

Canvas Art Prints
To turn your digital photos into art on canvas:
www.CanvasOnDemand.com
www.Costco.com

Clear Lidded Storage Bins
www.ContainerStore.com
www.OrganizeIt.com
www.Target.com

Decorative Folding Screens
www.EthanAllen.com
www.HomeDecorators.com

Kitchen Cooking Islands
www.eKitchenIslands.com
www.HomeDecorators.com
www.KitchenSource.com

Kitchen Pot Racks
www.HomeDecorators.com
www.JCPenney.com

Library Steps
www.Levenger.com

Melamine Cabinets
www.Target.com
www.WalMart.com

Office Chairs/Desks
www.HomeDecorators.com
www.OfficeDepot.com
www.Staples.com

Plastic Carrying Caddies
www.ContainerStore.com
www.Target.com
www.WalMart.com

RV Supplies
www.Amazon.com
www.ContainerStore.com
www.Magellans.com

Silk Plants
www.SilkFlowers.com
www.WalMart.com

Small Bistro Tables and Chairs
www.BallardDesigns.com
www.HomeGoods.com
www.Target.com

Stacking Storage Cubes and Crates
www.ContainerStore.com
www.OrganizeIt.com
www.Target.com

Storage Trunks
www.Pier1.com
www.Target.com

Velvet Clothing Hangers
www.OnlySlimlineHangers.com
www.Target.com
www.TJMaxx.com

YOUR SMALL SPACE NOTES

Foyers and More

Making a Grand Entrance

When you walk up to your small home space and into your front entrance, does its organized and cozy ambience make you breathe a sigh of relief that you're home, or do you feel angst because you're once again tripping over boots, mittens, the dog's leash, and yesterday's mail?

Launching Pad

No matter how small your home, and whether or not you have a "real" foyer, it's important to keep this space organized, functional, and pleasant as it's your life's landing and launching pad, *daily.* I agree with those who feel that an entryway's appearance is important from a functional viewpoint because it makes an immediate statement about how you live and who you are, but I disagree that your home's entrance should be designed to impress guests. Instead, it should be functional and pleasant *for you and your family*. You should be able to say "I'm so happy I'm home!" the minute you walk in your front door.

Outside-In

The organization and appearance of your front entryway or foyer really starts with the outside, *before* you even set foot in the front door. If you live in a house or townhouse with a walkway or sidewalk, is it in good shape? If not, repair or replace it and clean up any surrounding dead shrubs or flowers.

More Dash Than Cash

No matter how humble, it's easy to make your outside front entrance lovely with a little creativity and a few dollars. Hanging a colorful silk wreath on your front door and putting a couple of flower pots brimming with bright blooms on your front step will inexpensively transform your ho-hum entrance into an *aha!* one.

Front Steps and New Friends

You never know where an organized and pleasing front entrance may lead you. I remember as a young newlywed transforming the drab entryway of our first tiny home. Our house had a front stoop and three steps with cute lattice panels on either side to complement the white window shutters. Ours was the middle house of three little houses that all looked exactly the same, and around town they were humorously referred to as the "Three Little Pig" houses. To personalize the front of our home, Steve built three square wooden flower planters and I stained them a redwood color, filled them with bright pink geraniums, and set one on each step. At night in the summer I loved to sit on our front stoop with a glass of iced tea and a good book, and my little flower boxes became the conversation piece that helped me make a new friend of the young neighbor gal who moved in next door.

Twenty-five years later, when we bought a plain, one-level beige box of a condo not far from the beach, we turned our postage-stamp-sized front yard into a colorful cottage garden, complete with rows of beautiful pink and white impatiens lining our little walkway, lovely urns brimming with beautiful flowers on our front step, and a big floral wreath on our front door. The happiness it brought us was priceless, and my neighbor brought her adorable young son over daily to stop and smell the flowers.

Apartment Entrance Pizzazz

Don't think that just because you live in an apartment with a hallway that you can't organize and spruce up your "front walk." In my current high-rise apartment hallway, where each front door looks exactly like every other one, I placed a welcoming floral wreath on my front door (surprise, surprise!) and bought two adorable ceramic kitty statues to place in the corner next to my door. On the other side of the door I placed a silk potted plant with bright pink blooms. My neighbor down the hall stopped my husband one day and told him how much she enjoys walking past our front door! Like I hope yours does, my front entrance sets the tone for me to walk into my serene home space. (If you don't have a doorman or security guard, put only inexpensive items on or near your front door, such as a wreath or plant.)

Nook Look

If you have a little more room in your apartment hallway, you can do what I did in our last apartment home. Since we live in Southern California, our hallway was covered but open to the outdoors. We had a corner unit near the fire escape, so I had a big "nook" right outside my front door. I placed a decorative wrought-iron bench surrounded by urns of silk plants and flowers near my door to create a "garden spot." Another neighbor turned her front entry nook into a clever outdoor storage area by placing a beautiful wooden armoire just outside her door to store jackets and shoes. I could go on and on about the beautiful and clever front entrances I saw in this apartment complex, with the point being to get clever and create an inviting entrance for *your* home!

Fab Front Foyer

Now that you've organized and cleaned up your front walkway, it's time for us to go inside. The first question to ask yourself is, *How do I feel when I walk into my foyer, and how do I want to feel?* Since you're reading this book, I'm assuming you want your foyer to feel organized and pleasant, so let's get started.

Easy Entryway

The function and aesthetics of your foyer will depend entirely on your family's needs and tastes. While a creative and fun-loving family might enjoy hanging large decorative hooks with colorful tote bags for each family member, another family would much prefer elegant closed storage cabinets with a large beautiful sculpture on top. Adapt my suggestions and ideas below to do what works best *for you*.

Of Paint and Patches

To get started on organizing your foyer, do an audit of the existing space. By that I mean get rid of anything you don't want or need, just as you would when cleaning out a closet. Once your space is cleared, come up with an overall plan and look you want for your entryway *before* you do any shopping. Search through home catalogs and websites for visual ideas and products.

Assess your foyer's paint and flooring. If you decide to repaint the walls and ceilings, use a satin or semigloss paint finish as it's easier to keep clean with the swipe of a wet cloth. And in small spaces, the sheen helps reflect light and make the space appear larger.

A bold wallpaper will bring dramatic impact to the space, so limit art on the walls if you choose wallpaper.

If you want to cover up flooring that is outdated or worn, consider putting a colorful rug over it if you can't replace it just now. Be sure the rug has a nonskid back to avoid slipping. If or when you do decide to replace the flooring, make sure it will not be slippery.

Lighting Love

Do you want to come home to a light, bright, sunny foyer or one that is cozy and intimate? Choose your light fixtures accordingly. Choose a chandelier with many bulbs for a light and bright feeling and a dimmer corner floor lamp for a cozy ambience.

Let's Get Creative

If you're the creative, artsy sort who loves everything visual and at your fingertips, as I mentioned above, simply hanging large, sturdy, decorative hooks in your foyer, one for each family member, works well for coats and backpacks. Be sure to place kids' hooks at a height they can reach. Buy a big colorful tote bag for each family member, all in different colors. The bags can be easily removed from the hook when headed out the door, and when hanging they can hold school papers, schedules, and all life's daily needs for when you must venture out. Tote bags can be monogrammed for an even more fun and personalized look.

Buy a shoe storage cubby for storing shoes, hats, and small athletic items. A small trunk also works well for these items, and you can sit on top of it to tie your shoes. If you wear only fun shoes that look like art, an over-the-door shoe holder works great and your fashionable shoes will add a touch of glam to your foyer. For dirty boots, consider a boot tray to catch mud.

To personalize your creative family's entrance, frame your kids' artwork in large black frames and hang them above the hooks for a functional *and* fun entryway.

Fancy Meeting You Here

Perhaps instead of fun and creative, you want a foyer that's both organized *and* fancy. Go for a clean and uncluttered look, even if you like traditional decor. Place a demilune table (a table that looks like half of a round table) against the wall in your entrance. Choose one that has a drawer in front for your keys, and place a beautiful hinged decorative box on top to hold items such as your cell phone and outgoing mail. Hang an ornate mirror over the table or stand your favorite oil painting on it for a luxe look. Place two beautiful urns on either side of the table, one for umbrellas and one for shoes and canes. Complete your oh-so-chic little entryway with a monogrammed doormat.

Locker Lowdown

One of the biggest challenges I hear from people who live in small apartments and condos is that they don't have a real foyer or entrance but instead walk right into their living room. One functional entrance idea for creating a faux foyer and for organizing this type of space is to use attractive lockers with doors to house and hide your coats, umbrellas, and boots. Since the lockers are usually tall, narrow, and not too deep, if there's enough wall space, you can place one on either side of a matching bench so you can sit down to tie your shoes. If the bench has a hinged lid, you can store things like hats and mittens inside. Your local auto body shop can custom paint lockers for you.

Dresser Diva

Another attractive and functional way to organize your faux foyer is to place a small dresser or bedroom-style nightstand near your front door. The drawers can be used to store mittens, hats, and scarves. Since nightstands are low, they work great for storing kids' gear; if they are small enough, you can even use one for each child.

Handy Highboy

I don't have a formal foyer in my current high-rise apartment, so I walk right into my home's living area. Here's an idea I'd like to share with you. Just opposite my front door there's a little alcove in the wall. My hubby and I found a tall, antique-white, "shabby chic" style highboy dresser that fits perfectly in that little space, has many sizes of drawers, and with its curvy legs and beautiful carvings is a lovely piece of architectural detail as well. I store my table linens in it since it's close to our dining area, but it would work equally well for gloves, hats, mittens, keys, outgoing mail, and so forth. Think outside the box—this highboy dresser technically belongs in a bedroom, yet it's perfect as a foyer storage piece.

Keys, Mail, and Love Notes

I don't recommend processing your mail in the foyer as it's too easy to create a cluttered mess. Instead, immediately take your mail to your home office or kitchen paperwork space and do it there.

As for keys, it's great to keep them in your foyer so you always know where they are when you're headed out the door. Put them in your tote bag that you keep in the foyer, or put a hook on your purse like I do, hook the keys to the handle, and keep your purse in the foyer. Another solution is to store keys in the drawer of your foyer's dresser or nightstand or in a basket on top of it.

Hanging a bulletin board in your foyer can work well as a family message center if you don't mind visual stimulation there. Keys can also be hung on push pins, and any invitations, photos, or love notes for family members can be placed there.

Mirror Magic

I've already mentioned using mirrors in your foyer, but to create a truly dramatic effect, hang a large floor-to-ceiling mirror. Not only will it visually expand your space but you'll be able to check your darling "do" and new outfit before leaving for the day.

Coat Closet Kudos

If you're lucky enough to have a coat closet in your small space entry, hats off (pun intended) to you! My husband and I shared a standard-sized coat closet in our last apartment, so to give you ideas on how to organize your own, here's how we organized ours:

- We each took one half of the hanging rod for coats.
- On the shelf above the hanging rod we stacked clear plastic lidded drawers to hold our gloves, scarves, batteries, and light bulbs.
- Underneath the hanging rod stood his boots and our vacuum cleaner.
- An over-the-door clear plastic shoe holder held our shoes so that as soon as we entered our foyer we could remove them and put them away.
- Hooks mounted on the wall inside the closet held our broom, mop, and fire extinguisher.

Happy Hallway

I'm a firm believer in creating a "happy hallway" if you have one that's part of, or adjacent to, your front entrance. By that I mean turning your "plain vanilla" hallway into a lovely art gallery of memories. It doesn't have to cost a lot to do this. Enlarge favorite family photos to 8" × 10" size or larger, frame them all in matching black or white frames, and hang them collage-style. The same can be done with your children's artwork.

I love my own happy hallway wall. Whenever we travel, my husband and I buy a small painting or print by a local artist, and after thirty years we have several of them hanging collage-style on the wall near our front entrance, right above our little foyer table. We enjoy seeing them every day, and they're a conversation starter when guests visit.

I also love to visit my friends' home because after traveling to thirty-plus countries, they have created an artistic collage of their travels on the entire wall that extends from their front entrance along their living and dining rooms. Many a time I have enjoyed conversing about their art collection from around the world while we celebrated life together over a lovely dinner.

Back Door Guests Are Best

You've seen that famous plaque in stores that says *Back Door Guests Are Best*, right? So far I've focused on helping you get your front entrance or foyer organized. If your small space is large enough that you have both front and back entrances, you can use the same basic organizing principles I've just described, with the difference being to keep the front entrance a bit more formal and the back one a little more casual for everyday use.

Favorite Foyer

I'm so happy that by now you're on your way to creating an organized "favorite foyer" that's just right for you and your family. Remember, your entrance sets the tone to welcome you into the rest of your home.

Resources for Small Foyers

Armoires
www.BallardDesigns.com
www.EthanAllen.com
www.HomeDecorators.com

Boot Trays
www.BallardDesigns.com

Bulletin Boards
www.HomeDepot.com
www.Target.com
www.WalMart.com

Decorative Mirrors
www.BallardDesigns.com
www.HomeDecorators.com
www.Target.com

Decorative Wall Hooks
www.Target.com
www.WalMart.com

Demilune Tables
www.BallardDesigns.com
www.EthanAllen.com
www.HomeDecorators.com

Over-the-Door Clear Plastic Shoe Holders
www.ContainerStore.com
www.Target.com
www.WalMart.com

Shoe Storage Cubbies
www.ContainerStore.com
www.ShopGetOrganized.com
www.Target.com

Silk Wreaths
www.HomeGoods.com
www.Target.com
www.WalMart.com

Storage Lockers
www.JCPenney.com
www.PotteryBarn.com

Tote Bags
www.BallardDesigns.com (monogrammed)
www.LandsEnd.com (monogrammed)
www.Target.com

YOUR SMALL SPACE NOTES

6

Lovely Living
in a Small Living and/or
Family Room

Is your living room a formal and tidy place for entertaining company or for quietly reading a book on a fancy antique settee next to the fireplace? Is it a place where your kids are free to hang out with their friends on cushy casual sofas, play video games, and leave a popcorn kernel or two on the floor? Or perhaps your room falls somewhere in between?

Because today's lifestyles tend to be more casual than in the past, and because this is a book about small home spaces that likely don't have separate living and family rooms, I'm going to give you ideas as if you use just one room for both functions. My first question to you is: How would you like your living/family room to look, to feel, and to function?

Remember those three key words—*look, feel,* and *function.*

Dream Time

Before you start reorganizing and rearranging your room, you'll want to do some dreaming. So once again, get out your three-ring binder. Buy some home decor magazines and catalogs and start clipping. As you look the rooms over from page to page, you'll start to see themes emerge of organizing and arranging ideas that *look* good to you. Cut out pictures of any living/family "dream rooms" that you like.

If you prefer to save the photos on your computer rather than in a binder, type "living/family room organizing and decorating" into your search engine and use the "Save Picture As" function on the toolbar. Set up a folder called "Living Room," then drag and drop your sample dream room photos in there. You can also print the photos and put them in your binder if you like. Even if I keep the photos on my computer, I personally prefer the binder because I like to make notes on the photos about where I might be able to buy a particular item. I can also take the binder with me when I shop.

Once you've gathered all your dream room photos, look them over carefully. What makes the room *feel* organized and homey to you? Remember when looking at magazine and catalog photos that they've been staged for photography purposes, but you can adapt the ideas to your own home in a way that *functions* well for your room and family.

Decluttering Diva

When you've determined the look, feel, and function that you want your own living/family room to have, it's then time to declutter your existing living room. (No, it's not time to go shopping just yet!) Look around your room and decide which items you no longer want to keep. Be ruthless because in a small space, less is more. Ditch old newspapers and magazines, and donate any knickknacks that are no longer the look you want for your new room. Ditto for the art on your walls.

Fine Furnishings and Accessories

Next, evaluate your existing furnishings and functional accessories. Keep function in mind as you decide which pieces to keep and which ones to get rid of, and opt for pieces that will support your room as a comfortably organized space. Also remember to consider how you and your family *use* the room and plan accordingly. If you have game night every Friday night, you'll want a game table and chairs. Or if like my hubby and me you prefer Friday night as your "curl up and get cozy" at-home movie night, be sure to include comfy sofa seating that's facing your entertainment center.

Fresh Upholstery

As you evaluate your furnishings, if they're worn, consider reupholstering or having them cleaned and covering them with a fresh new slipcover. Keep in mind that reupholstering furniture is almost always nearly as expensive as buying a new piece, so decide accordingly. Slipcovers can be costly too, but the wonderful thing about them is they're washable. This year I bought a new white slipcovered sofa that I absolutely adore, and washing the slipcover is a breeze. Incidentally, if you do decide to buy a new sofa rather than reupholster or slipcover the old one, a sofa is one of two pieces of furniture in your home (the other being your bed) that I consider an investment, so buy the absolute best quality you can find and save money elsewhere in your décor.

Painting Fun

Conceal scratches on wooden furniture legs or tabletops with a furniture touch-up pen, or have your pieces repainted. As long as a piece is sturdy and in otherwise good condition, I'm a big advocate of repainting because it's a cost-effective way to freshen up a room. Just this past year, since I am gradually redecorating my whole home in shades of white and neutrals, I had several favorite pieces of wooden furniture professionally repainted and I love how they turned out. Be sure to use one of the new no-VOC paints to keep your room free from harmful chemicals to help keep your family healthy. To paint metal furniture, try your local auto body shop. (Unless you're a real whiz with a paintbrush, I don't recommend painting either wooden or metal furniture yourself. *I speak from experience.*) And while we're on the topic of paint, be sure to check your walls to see if they need freshening up and choose a shade of paint you absolutely adore!

Furniture Shopping

Once you've decided which furnishings and functional accessories you no longer want, decide what pieces you need to replace. Make a list in your notebook with an estimated dollar amount next to each item so you stay within your budget.

Go through home goods catalogs and search online for styles and prices. Don't forget to think "function first" for furniture and evaluate each piece accordingly, remembering that in small spaces every inch counts.

Listed below are some good functional furnishings and accessories to keep or buy.

Bookcase Beauty

Floor-to-ceiling bookcases work wonderfully not just for books but for artful displays of pottery and sculpture because they make the room appear larger and because they draw the eye upward. They're also handy for storing games and videos, and to put brightly colored bins or baskets on for kids' toys. If you're worried about dust, buy bookcases with glass doors.

Painting the backs of your bookcases a favorite color will make your art pop. I recall visiting my favorite interior designer's home and noticing that several of the bookcases she used to display her colorful china had backs that were painted bright yellow, soft blue, and lime green. Those colors vibrantly showcased her beautiful dishes. And I recently visited a historic hotel and walked past a beautifully carved bookcase with the back painted a soft medium green that artfully showcased several ornate white urns on its shelves. Stunning!

In other words, when you're deciding how to organize your home don't be afraid to also add a little pizzazz to it!

Trunk and Ottoman Time

Ottomans with hinged lids make great coffee tables, as do antique trunks and end tables with shelves. They provide extra space for books and magazines. Coffee tables with a shelf on the bottom work well for the same.

Suitcase Serenade

Antique suitcases or stacked trunks also work great as end tables on either side of your sofa and can do double duty for holding games, puzzles, blankets, and so on. Plus, they add cozy charm to your room.

Amazing Armoires

Armoires are super for housing and hiding the TV. Many are made with a cutout in the back specifically for cords and have lower shelves to hold DVD players and home stereo equipment.

Bountiful Baskets

Baskets make a living/family room feel warm and comfy. They are also great for storing books, magazines, and knitting or other craft projects. I have baskets of books on either side of my sofa and love the nice ambience they give my room.

Built-In Benches

Built-in benches work great as seating in a corner with a game table. One home we lived in had a family room with built-in benches that had hinged lids. I stored extra blankets and sheets in them for the nearby sleeper sofa. You could also store games in the bench.

Gracious Living Room (a.k.a. "Guest Room")

If you need to use your small living/family room for guests, never fear. Simply buy a sleeper sofa instead of a regular sofa.

Store your sheets and blankets in the ottoman or trunk that you're using as a coffee table and place a folding screen in the corner to hide guests' luggage. Set up a basket of towels and toiletries they can carry to the bathroom, and place a breakfast tray on the coffee table or ottoman so they'll feel welcome.

Control Remote Controls

What to do with all those remote controls? One simple and inexpensive solution is to buy decorative wooden boxes for the top of your coffee table. I bought two of them in different sizes and stacked them on top of each other. One holds our remotes and the other holds my hubby's headset that he prefers to wear while watching TV.

Beautiful Built-Ins

I once interviewed a family about their small home for a magazine article, and they had built-in cabinetry in their living room to house all their media equipment. They told me it was built by carpenters who usually construct boat cabinets. The family hired them figuring if they could make built-ins to fit in a boat, they could do it for their small home. Great idea!

Furniture Arrangement

Once you've evaluated your room's functional furnishings and accessories needs and have purchased any new pieces, you'll want to arrange them comfortably. Here are some good small room furniture arrangement options:

Square Conversation Area

This arrangement works well because it offers a cozy conversation area, as well as a nice area for reading and watching TV or movies.

- Place your sofa/loveseat along one long living room wall and your TV on a shelf on the opposite wall with tall bookcases on either side of it.
- Place a coffee table in front of your sofa.
- Place end tables against each end of your sofa and put lamps on them for reading lighting.
- Place two chairs near either end of your sofa, facing the coffee table.
- An area rug underneath the coffee table anchors the space.

Loveseat Opposite Option

Place two loveseats facing each other (away from the wall) with a coffee table between them. If you have a fireplace, it's nice to place them facing each other in front of the fireplace.

Four Chairs Option

If you don't mind not being able to lie down on a sofa, place four club chairs facing each other with a coffee table in between.

Sectional Sofas

I don't often recommend sectional sofas for small living rooms because they usually come in such large sizes that they just don't work well. However, www.BallardDesigns.com carries smaller sectional sofas that are also attractive. Sectionals work great if you have kids as they tend to be family friendly and more casual than other furnishing styles or arrangements.

Lighting Love

Be sure you have adequate and functional lighting in your living room. Task lighting for reading and crafts is important, and I like arched floor lamps on either end of the sofa because they can be adjusted to needed height. Or use end table lamps rather than overhead lighting.

Easy Entertaining

It's great fun to entertain friends and extended family, and I'm a firm believer you shouldn't avoid doing so just because you live in a small home. On the contrary, attitude is everything and you just have to get a bit more creative to entertain in a small living room.

Beautiful Buffet

Many a time I have entertained in my small living room by setting up a beautiful buffet in the adjacent kitchen/dining area and then eating in the living/family room area. You don't have to have a buffet or buffet table to do this. In my little 922-square-foot beach condo, my washer and dryer were adjacent to the kitchen counter, so I simply draped a long stretch of beautiful fabric over both the counter and the washer and dryer and set out platters filled with gorgeous food. We provided lap trays at one end of the buffet, then took our trays into the living room to eat and had a fine time!

Another time in a different apartment I put all the leaves in my antique rectangular Duncan Phyfe table, extending it into a long buffet table. I topped it with a colorful sheet that I tied in pretty knots at each end and added ribbons. We set a colorful punch bowl in the middle, placed trays of beautiful food around it, and once again took our lap trays into the nearby living room to sit and eat and have great conversation. Presentation is everything when entertaining in a small space.

Card Table Cuisine

If you prefer not to eat on lap trays in your living room, set up several card tables covered with pretty tablecloths. You can arrange them as individual food stations with different types of food for different colored tablecloths. Place four card tables end to end to create one long table to sit at. Or you can put four of them in a square to create one large table in the middle of your living room.

Festive Small Living Room Feast

I remember one especially memorable feast at the small condo of some good friends. Their dining table was pulled out into the middle of the living room, and they put several leaves in it to accommodate about twelve guests. The hostess was dressed in a gorgeous outfit, and she had set the table most beautifully with fine china and linens, place cards with everyone's names written on them, beautiful crystal glasses, candles, and a festive Thanksgiving centerpiece. I thought we were dining at the Ritz! The point here is that the joy of being happily together around a beautiful table in your small living room is precious time spent together, so get creative and enjoy it!

Living and Family Room Farewell

I hope I've given you both practical and creative ideas for getting your small family/living room organized and arranged for your maximum comfort. Enjoy! Now let's move on to the next room in your home.

Resources for Small Living/Family Rooms

Antique Suitcases
www.eBay.com

Baskets
www.Michaels.com
www.Target.com

Bookcases
www.EthanAllen.com
www.HomeDecorators.com
www.Ikea.com
www.Levenger.com

Card Tables
www.Target.com
www.WalMart.com

Furnishings/Accessories Catalogs
www.BallardDesigns.com
www.EthanAllen.com
www.HomeDecorators.com

Lap Trays
www.TheFind.com
www.Target.com

No-VOC Paint
www.BenjaminMoore.com
www.BioshieldPaint.com
www.Sherwin-Williams.com

Slipcovers
www.CozyCottageSlipcovers.com
www.SureFit.net

Sofas, Sleeper Sofas, Loveseats, Small Sectional Sofas
www.BallardDesigns.com
www.EthanAllen.com

Storage Ottomans and Trunks
www.HomeDecorators.com
www.Target.com

Wood Furniture Touch-Up Kit (for scratches)
www.AceHardware.com
www.OfficeDepot.com

YOUR SMALL SPACE NOTES

Kitchen and Dining Delights

Organize Your Kitchen and Dining Room for Delicious Dining

Is there any other room in a home like the kitchen that evokes instant emotion in us as human beings? What comes to mind when you hear the word *kitchen*? Do you think of sleek white designer cabinets that hold elegant china for your fancy dinner parties? Maybe you envision a cozy country kitchen with baskets hanging from the ceiling and hot cider simmering on the stove. Or perhaps you picture a tiny utilitarian galley kitchen in an urban high-rise where not much else is cooked up other than frozen TV dinners.

Savvy Small Kitchens

Small kitchens can either feel oppressively claustrophobic or functionally handy. Let's opt for making yours efficiently organized, like an airplane cockpit, where everything you need to do the job is right at your fingertips. We won't get into designing a brand-new kitchen here; instead we'll do our best to organize the one you already have.

Assess Your Space

The first step in getting your kitchen in tip-top organizing shape is to assess your existing space and determine if it's meeting your meal prep, dining, and aesthetic needs. And never fear, you *can* do a lot to improve your kitchen storage and organization, even if your kitchen is teeny tiny.

For example, when I was a newlywed, our miniscule galley kitchen (can you say *cozy*?) was about 6′ × 8′, if that. We quickly took inventory of our storage needs before putting our wedding gifts away in the cabinets, and here's what we did to make it an efficiently organized space.

My hubby built a nice white cabinet at the end of my sink for pots and pans and canned goods, which also gave me extra counter space. We hung a wooden pot rack behind the stove and put hooks on the wall next to it to hang cooking utensils. Round wire baskets hung in the corner above the refrigerator to store potatoes and onions, a basket on top of the refrigerator housed paper plates and napkins, and I put my new set of colorful canisters for flour and sugar (a wedding gift) on the counter behind my dish drainer. Three tiny shelves above my sink held pretty containers for tea, coffee, and sugar cubes, and baskets on top of the cabinets held extra groceries. We repainted the Pepto Bismol pink walls a bright semigloss white that significantly brightened the room and was easy to keep clean. I sewed rug squares together to make a colorful patchwork rug for our kitchen. The final touch was a new curtain on the window and—presto . . . in just a few days, our tiny kitchen was both functional and cheerful. We hosted many a dinner with new friends in that home. *You can do the same!*

Inventory Time

Below are some questions to ask as you take inventory of your small kitchen. As you read them, think about how you can problem-solve for your own kitchen's challenges.

- How many cabinets do you have and are they currently meeting all your cookware and grocery storage needs?
- Do your cabinets go all the way to the ceiling? If not, are you using the possible storage or display space on top?
- Do you have a pantry and is it adequate in size?
- How many drawers do you have and are there enough?
- Do you have an oven drawer that you are using to store cookware?
- Do you have adequate under-the-counter storage beneath your sink?
- Is there adequate lighting?
- Is your refrigerator a good size for the room?

- Do you have or want a dishwasher, and if so, is there room for one?

Storage Solutions

Probably the biggest challenge in organizing a small kitchen is storage. Therefore, it's very important to make sure you don't buy groceries, utensils, or cookware that you aren't really going to use. As I mentioned earlier in chapter 3, my best small kitchen organizing tip of all time is this: *buy only white dishes and clear glassware.* Mix and match different styles and if you break a piece, you won't have to buy a whole new set. Food looks simply scrumptious on white dishes! I cleaned out my cupboards last year, donating to charity any dishes that were not all white or clear glass, and I've never once looked back.

Kitchen Organizing Tips

After living with thirteen different small kitchens over thirty years (*yes, really!*), below are my best tips for organized kitchens:

- It bears repeating: only buy all-white dishes and clear glassware for a uniform look. One set to serve eight to twelve people will do, and buy a style that you like to use for both everyday and for entertaining. If you crave color, dress them up with colorful napkins, napkin rings, and tablecloths.

- Don't buy more plastic leftover storage containers than you really need. Store the ones you have by nesting them inside each other and keeping the lids next to them in a shoebox without the lid.
- Speaking of shoeboxes, they work great for storing small items like spices and gravy mixes.
- Plastic turntables work well for holding spices or small condiments in the refrigerator.
- It's okay to store cookware in your bottom stove drawer, but be careful about storing it in the oven unless every family member knows it's there. You don't want to turn the oven on with cookware still in it.
- Compartmentalize your junk/utility drawer by arranging checkbook boxes inside it. A plastic silverware tray or a muffin tin also works well.
- Think of your refrigerator like another cabinet and organize it accordingly. Fruit goes in drawers, condiments in the doors, and label clear plastic containers of food.
- Organize your pantry according to types of food. All cereals together, all canned goods together, and so on. Use small baskets or shoeboxes for small items like gum and gravy mixes.
- Remove cereals and crackers from their original packaging and store them in clear plastic containers.
- Install hooks inside your cabinets to hang your mugs, which will save room on the shelves.

- Mount an under-the-cabinet glass holder for long-stemmed glasses.
- Use a roll-out trash can under your sink and store the extra trash bags in the bottom.
- A plastic carrying caddy with a handle on top works well under the kitchen sink for holding your cleaning supplies.
- Metal grids hung on the wall with S hooks work great for holding pans and cooking utensils.
- Keep your knives at your fingertips while cooking by using a wooden knife block. I keep mine near the kitchen stove.
- It's better not to do your paperwork in the kitchen as it can become a clutter area. Use a desk in your living room or home office area instead.
- Hang a magnetized memo pad on the refrigerator to keep a running list of needed grocery items.
- Go through your cabinets every six months to get rid of any chipped or damaged dishes or cookware and replace them.
- Buy the best cookware you can afford so it looks nice if you hang it on a pot rack.
- Store pet food in metal or plastic containers with lids.
- Plastic dishpans work great in the fridge or a cupboard as an extra "drawer." I store fruit in my fridge this way.
- Buy small appliances that can be mounted under the cabinets to save counter space.

- Mount your microwave over the stove to save space if at all possible, rather than having it on the counter.
- Use colorful canisters to hold your flour, sugar, tea, and coffee and add a bit of colorful ambience to your small space.
- Mount spice racks on the back of your cabinet doors to save cabinet space.
- Hang colorful plates on your walls instead of pictures.
- If you have room, paint an old dresser and use it as a kitchen island. The drawers can hold dishtowels and cloths, and you can mount your paper towel holder and hooks for cooking utensils on one end. Have a piece of granite or glass custom cut to fit the top.
- A magnetized stainless steel strip mounted to the wall next to your stove works well for holding sharp knives, but be careful if you have children.
- Open shelves should be kept organized so they don't look cluttered. All-white dishes and clear glassware and colorful pottery in different styles look especially attractive on open shelves.
- Mount a cabinet door rack on the inside of your cabinet to hold your plastic wrap, aluminum foil, and storage bags.
- Over-the-door shoe holders on the back of a pantry door can hold spices, sauce mix packets, chewing gum, and so forth.
- A stacking corner shelf rack works great for creating more space for your dinner plates.

- Remove the doors from the front of your cabinets and paint the insides of the cabinets your favorite color to showcase your white dishes.
- Install shelves in a small armoire and use it as a pantry.
- A strawberry jar from your favorite garden center works great on your countertop for wooden spoons and rolling pin storage.
- Antique trophy cups are fun for storing large cooking utensils.
- Shoeboxes or baskets store candles well.
- Garden pots and urns work great to store cooking utensils upright.
- Hang a large mirror on one wall to amplify light.
- Put tubular lighting underneath your cabinets for soft ambience.
- If you can install a skylight in your kitchen, it will add wonderful natural lighting.
- Small outdoor bistro tables work well as breakfast or snack tables.
- If you don't have a kitchen window, mount a rectangular planter on the wall over your sink and "plant" it with silk geraniums.
- Hang a painting of an outdoor scene above your sink to give the feeling that you're looking out a window.
- In one of my small kitchens, I used a tall baker's rack for displaying plants, dish towels, and colorful canisters. A plant shelf would work equally well.

- Rolling carts make handy kitchen islands and you can store supplies on the bottom shelf.
- A folding butcher block table can be used as a kitchen island and stored next to the refrigerator when not in use.
- Buy large clear glass jars with lids for storing things such as rice, beans, and cereals.
- Plastic turntables are dandy for storage and easy access of medicines and supplements.
- Put lights inside your glass-fronted kitchen cabinets to make your glassware sparkle.
- If you have room, a freestanding kitchen island with shelves adds extra storage and food prep space.
- All-white or off-white cabinets, walls, and ceiling make a small kitchen appear larger.
- Hang a large pot rack in the center of your galley kitchen for ease of use and for a cozy French country look.
- Use baskets to corral your cookbooks.
- A three-ring binder nicely holds photocopied recipes inside clear plastic page protectors.
- Store your dishes and cutlery near the dishwasher for ease of unloading.
- Consider plate rack slots for easy access to plates and for a nice decorative look.
- Remove the front doors of one cabinet and create your own coffee bar by housing your coffeemaker, cups, and coffee there.

- If you have a small coat closet near your kitchen, install shelves and use it as a pantry instead.
- Place a muffin tin inside your junk drawer to separate keys, rubber bands, and other miscellaneous items.
- Categorize your box of recipe cards alphabetically by topic. Mine holds recipes exchanged with friends over thirty years, and the memories we have shared together through those meals are one of my greatest life treasures.

Going Green

As you organize your kitchen, allow space for recycling. It doesn't have to be complicated. I simply placed two trash cans in the cabinet under my kitchen sink. One holds trash and the other holds plastic bottles and paper for recycling. You can also purchase plastic stacking bins designed especially for recycling. See the list of resources at the end of this chapter.

Dining and Entertaining with Ease

Most small homes, apartments, and condos don't have a separate dining room per se. Instead, a space off the kitchen serves as a dining area. That doesn't mean, however, that you can't enjoy your dining area both alone and with your family, plus have wonderful large dinner gatherings there. My hubby and I have been fond of entertaining various size groups of friends over the years, and we've had to get very creative. We've also had a lot of fun at the same time!

Entertaining Organizing Tip

I always recommend that you cook and prepare ahead of time when you have a small kitchen and dining room, as there's not really room to be cooking together while you visit. Plus, moving pots and pans around while your guests are there can be noisy as well as exhausting for you in a small space. Much better to do it all in advance, then take a nap, get yourself gussied up, turn on some wonderful music, and enjoy your guests!

Dining Faux Pas

While it's great to be so organized that you do everything before your dinner guests arrive, dining faux pas do happen to the savviest of hosts and hostesses. All any of us can do is make light of it and laugh.

Even though I've been entertaining for thirty years, probably my most embarrassing moment as a hostess was just this past year. Steve and I invited a sweet couple we had just met to dinner in our home. I planned, organized, and cooked everything ahead of time, including the tasty squash soup simmering in the slow cooker. Imagine my horror when I noticed the man sitting opposite me at our round table was not eating the soup, and the rest of us were almost done. Suddenly I realized he wasn't eating because I had forgotten to put a bowl of soup in front of him! Gentleman that he was, he never said a word, and he was more than kind when I realized my error. Since he had a great sense of humor, we all had a good laugh!

More Organized Dining Ideas

Here are some tips that you can adapt to your own space.

Newlywed Entertaining

In our first tiny newlywed nest we had a large rectangular table in the corner of the living room, just off the kitchen. We stored its leaves in the closet until company came, and then we pulled the table out, put a pretty tablecloth on it, and pulled chairs from other rooms for our guests. Sometimes we used the table to set a buffet. Even with that tiny dining area, I hosted a bridal shower for my best friend when she got married, and it was a delight for all of us just to be together and make memories. Another time we invited an elderly lady we met at church to join us for Thanksgiving dinner since she had no family. She beamed with happiness and recounted the story to others time and again about how much she enjoyed her time in our little home.

What acquaintance can you turn into a friend today by inviting them to your small home for fun and fellowship?

Drop Leaf Dining Table

As I mentioned earlier, I had a small drop leaf Duncan Phyfe antique table in my kitchen dining area for years. It had two additional leaves that could be put in to easily convert from a table for two to a table for twelve. We used that table for sit-down dinners as well as for buffets.

Bistro Dining

Do you like those quaint open-air bistro restaurants as much as I do? Then why not create the same feeling at home? It's a perfect way to enhance a small dining area. I did this in my square dining nook just off the small kitchen in my current urban high-rise. The base of my round glass-topped designer table looks like white tree branches, and recently I found some gorgeous copper-colored metal bistro chairs with scroll backs. My hubby re-covered the seats in an elegant floral-embossed white fabric. The airiness of the glass-topped table combined with the open scrollwork on the chairs creates a garden-like bistro feel that everyone comments about.

Military Thanksgiving

What memorably special meal have you organized and celebrated in your small kitchen and dining room? One Thanksgiving my hubby and I popped up the leaves on our Duncan Phyfe table in the small dining area of our little beach condo. We set a festive table and hosted three Marines for dinner. They came to our home as complete strangers through a church program, and three hours of fellowship later they all left as friends.

More Dining Delights

Here are a few more final tips and ideas for organized and artful dining in your small space dining area:

- Clear glass tables enlarge a space.
- Round dining tables foster intimacy but are limited in how many people they can seat. The exception is a wooden table with leaves that can be inserted to expand it.
- Banquette seating in a corner, with benches on the opposite side of a rectangular table, saves space.

- Round stools save space.
- Open, scroll-back metal chairs give the illusion of space more than solid wooden chairs.
- If you play games at your dining table, choose a square table with a drawer.
- You can get more chairs around a round table with a pedestal base.
- Armless dining chairs give more elbow room and have a sleeker look.
- An area rug under your dining table reduces noise.
- Hang a large mirror on an end wall in your dining area to visually increase the space and to reflect light.
- Place a long, twelve-inch-deep, rectangular Parsons table against the end wall of your dining room and store entertaining items underneath it in decorative baskets.
- Line one wall of your dining area with twelve-inch-deep bookshelves from floor to ceiling to feel like you are dining in a cozy library.
- Attractive folding chairs can be leaned up against the wall for architectural interest. I have two white antique folding chairs against my dining room wall that nicely achieve this effect.

Small Space Wisdom

Entertaining friends in my home is one of the joyous occasions in my life, and I have never been willing to give up entertaining guests just because I've lived in small spaces. I hope I have encouraged you to do the same.

Always remember that it's far more important to have a kind spirit of hospitality and friendship as the emphasis of your home, rather than neglect to invite others to visit you there just because you lack large rooms or expensive furnishings. A true home is really about the size of your heart, not about the size of your space.

Resources for Small Kitchens and Dining Areas

Baker's Racks
www.ContainerStore.com
www.Michaels.com

Cabinet Door Racks
www.ContainerStore.com
www.ShopGetOrganized.com

Canisters
www.HomeGoods.com
www.Target.com

Freestanding Kitchen Islands
www.AllKitchenCarts.com
www.ChefsResource.com
www.KitchenEmporium.com
www.KitchenSource.com

Hanging Vegetable Baskets
www.ContainerStore.com
www.UsefulThings.com

Magnetized Memo Pads
www.Target.com
www.WalMart.com

Metal Wall Grids and S Hooks
www.Organize.com

Outdoor Bistro Tables
www.HomeGoods.com
www.Target.com

Over-the-Door Shoe Holders
www.ShopGetOrganized.com
www.Target.com

Parsons Tables
www.RoomandBoard.com
www.WestElm.com

Pet Food Storage Bins
www.BallardDesigns.com
www.Target.com

Plastic Carrying Caddies
www.ContainerStore.com
www.ShopGetOrganized.com

Plastic Turntables
www.Target.com
www.WalMart.com

Portable Pantries
www.ComfortChannel.com
www.ShopGetOrganized.com

Pot Racks
www.BallardDesigns.com
www.JCPenney.com

Recycling Bins
www.Amazon.com
www.ImprovementsCatalog.com
www.LNT.com

Rollout Trash Cans
www.ContainerStore.com
www.Target.com

Stacking Corner Shelf for Plates
www.ContainerStore.com
www.ShopGetOrganized.com

Strawberry Jars
www.ArmstrongGarden.com

Tubular Lighting
www.HomeDepot.com
www.Target.com

Under-the-Counter Glassware Holders
www.ContainerStore.com

Wooden Knife Blocks
www.CrateandBarrel.com
www.Target.com

--- YOUR SMALL SPACE NOTES ---

8

Bathroom Bliss

*Organizing Your Small Bathroom for a
Spa-Like Experience*

Recently Steve and I toured some beautiful new homes with bathrooms the size of our living room. (We love to go on new construction open house tours to get decorating ideas for our own home.) I imagined how much fun it would be to sink down into one of those big oval Jacuzzi tubs, drink a glass of iced tea in a long-stemmed crystal glass, and luxuriate in a deep, warm bubble bath. And then of course when I was all done, I'd pamper myself by putting on my makeup and doing my hair at my mile-long, custom-made vanity!

But alas, since most of us who live in small spaces don't have the luxury of an oversized Jacuzzi tub in a bathroom the size of most people's living rooms, nor do we have a personal marble-topped primping station, we have to get creative in order to create our own mini-spa experience.

Even if your bathroom is ultra-tiny, I'm a firm believer that not only *can* you create a serene and organized bathroom, but you *should* strive to do so. After a long hard day, there's nothing that soothes the aching body and tired mind like a warm bubble bath, some favorite soft music, French milled soaps, and a plush cozy towel, all of which can easily become part of even the tiniest bathroom.

Yes, I do realize that your kids' rubber duckies and their wet towels on the floor don't exactly remind you of a deluxe bathroom at a Four Seasons resort. But I also know that with some clever organizing and storage tips—and some family bathroom etiquette—you *can* create your very own serenely organized and efficient bathroom, and sooner than you might think.

So come on, I'm going to once again share with you some of the organizing strategies, ideas, and solutions I've personally used over the years.

Jacuzzi Train Tub

By now you're familiar with the tiny 20′ × 20′ home we rented when we were just newlyweds. After we finished organizing the kitchen and painting over the Pepto Bismol pink walls, we began making our miniscule bathroom an organized and restful place we could both enjoy. I loved its antique claw-foot tub, and imagine my delight when the whole thing vibrated and the water rippled all on its own the first time I took a bath! We lived across the street from a train track, and guess what? When the train whistle blew, our little house shook and my bathtub was indeed turned into a "Jacuzzi spa"—every night at precisely nine o'clock!

All fun aside, here's what we did in that little bathroom that will give you ideas to make yours organized, efficient, and pleasant:

- Any changes we made had to be temporary since we were renters, so we were careful about our budget and came up with a plan before we ever bought anything. I recommend you and your mate/family sit down together and brainstorm, writing the ideas in your notebook. Also, come up with a plan and a list before you ever set foot in a store to buy any organizing bins or decorative items.

- Our bathroom had cold linoleum on the floor, so we bought a plush carpet remnant and Steve laid it himself. This is not hard to do, but be sure you measure the room accurately before heading off to the home store. Bathroom carpet is not for everyone, but it works well in a rental situation because it can be easily removed when you move.

- We were blessed with a gorgeous porcelain pedestal sink to match our antique claw-foot bathtub. I bought fabric and sewed skirts for both of them. We stored extra toilet paper and tissues out of sight behind the skirts. If there's room, you could also put a cabinet or bookcase on either side of your pedestal sink to store towels and toiletry items.

- We were lucky enough to have a big built-in cabinet in one corner, and we used shoeboxes, plastic turntables, and silverware trays to sort toiletries inside it.

- We kept things like toothbrushes, toothpaste, and eye solutions in the medicine cabinet above the sink. Each of us took three shelves as our own. Giving each family member their own medicine cabinet shelf works great and you can label the shelves by first name.
- Since I love to read while soaking in a bubble bath, I bought a big round wicker basket to hold my magazines and placed it beside the tub.
- My hubby mounted decorative hooks near the sink and we hung our hairdryer and my curling iron on them so they were handy.
- We hung two towel bars and we each chose different towel colors so we knew whose was whose.
- We painted the walls a bright white using semigloss paint. I recommend semigloss paint for bathrooms because it's easy to wipe off and tolerates moisture well. Be sure to use nontoxic, no-VOC paint.
- Being a young and frugal new bride, I found some cute wicker fish at a discount store, spray-painted them, and hung them on the wall. Be careful not to hang any fine artwork or metal-framed paintings in your bathroom as the moisture will damage your art over time.
- Last but not least, we bought a new white roller shade and a pretty curtain since the neighbor's window looked right into ours. Check your window situation to be sure no one can see inside your bathroom.

Bathroom Bliss Tips

As you look around your small bathroom, there's always *something* you can do to improve it organizationally. My number one organizing tip is . . . you guessed it, *declutter*! Here's how:

- Clean out your medicine cabinet and get rid of any old medicines (which are better stored in the pantry or kitchen anyway), expired sunscreens, old toothbrushes, outdated makeup, and so forth.

- Wipe the cabinet shelves with a wet cloth and then wipe again with a dry one so there's no moisture.

- Evaluate your towel supply and replace any tattered ones with the softest, plushest comfort towels you can find! It works great to mount a decorative towel hook for each family member and for each person to also have their own towel color. Two complete towel sets per family member are sufficient. You can even assign one color per family member for things like toothbrushes and combs. That way when someone leaves something out, you'll know whose it is.

- Each family member's towels and toiletries don't necessarily have to be stored in the bathroom. Provide a wicker or plastic basket for each person and have them keep it in their bedroom, bringing it to the bathroom only when needed. They can even keep their towel on a hook behind the door in their bedroom.

- Get rid of any old shampoos, conditioners, and soaps. If you insist on keeping all the hotel sample soaps and shampoo bottles from when you travel, put them in a decorative basket near the shower so you use them up. Better yet, you could leave them at the hotel or donate them to a homeless shelter.

- Assign each family member one shelf in the medicine cabinet.
- Remove anything from the bathroom that is not related to grooming or creating a relaxing mini-spa experience.

Savvy Bathroom Storage

Small bathrooms are notoriously lacking in storage, but that doesn't mean you can't rectify the situation with some clever purchases. Here are some tried-and-true solutions:

- Think vertical and go up to the ceiling as much as you can with shelving and cabinetry.
- Buy an over-the-toilet cabinet and use it to store items such as shampoos and conditioners.
- Evaluate your toilet paper and tissue needs. It's hard to buy big bulk size packages of toilet paper for a small bathroom unless you have room to store them in another area of the house. Better to just buy a week's supply when grocery shopping and store it under your vanity.
- Narrow wire roll-out carts work great in tight spaces—for instance, near the tub—for holding towels, shampoos, and so forth. Narrow shelves ordinarily made to house CDs and DVDs also work well.

- Glass shelves hung on the wall are an efficient and attractive way to store towels, and they give the illusion of space more than wooden shelves do.

- Towel rings or hooks take up less space than towel bars.

- Shoeboxes help to compartmentalize under-the-vanity storage of toiletries. Plastic dishpans also do the job.

- Use silverware trays in your vanity drawers for sorting items such as toothbrushes, dental floss, and razors. Be careful to keep the safety lid on razors.

- Clear plastic over-the-door shoe holders work great for holding bathroom supplies. I once stayed in a cottage rental with a miniscule bathroom where you could barely turn around. Since there were no shelves, the first thing I did was buy one of these shoe holders and hang it on the outside of the shower curtain to store my toiletries. Problem solved for just a few dollars!

- Ah, remember those rubber duckies we talked about earlier? Hang fabric mesh bags on suction cups in the corner of your shower or tub and put the toys in there. If you'd prefer to teach your kids to put the toys away themselves, buy small plastic bins with drainage holes and store them in the tub.

- When I redecorated my bathroom in all-white this past year, I bought several small white vases and pitchers. I stood my hair gel and hand lotion in the vases and put my reading glasses in a pitcher. Another pitcher holds my cell phone while it's recharging.

- I bought a white china serving tray to use on my hubby's bathroom vanity to hold his keys, eyeglasses, and the love notes I write him on index cards.
- Pump soap dispensers are always neater and more sanitary than soap dishes.
- Clear glass containers with lids attractively hold cotton balls and prevent them from getting dusty.
- I use a clear antique spoon holder to store Q-tips. I have also put them in an antique floral creamer that was just the right size.
- Look around your kitchen for containers that would look attractive on your bathroom vanity and double as storage. A stemmed glass looks pretty holding Q-tips or soaps. However, be careful with glass in the bathroom if you have children.
- Buy a wicker basket for next to the tub and put rolled-up towels in it.
- Wire hangers that attach over the shower faucet hold shampoos and conditioners well.
- Buy a toilet bowl brush that's housed in a plastic container and store it by the toilet.
- Buy a shampoo and liquid soap dispenser that mounts in your shower to avoid soap slivers and slime.
- A baker's rack or bookcase works great for storing towels and other toiletries.
- Keep a step stool in the bathroom. If there's not enough room, keep it in a nearby hallway so your young kids can reach the sink and get ready on their own.

- An antique music cabinet works great for displaying and storing towels.
- Place a birdbath next to the tub to hold pretty soaps and small shampoo bottles.
- Candles give nice ambience to the bathroom, but be careful of using them if you have small children or pets.
- If you have room, an antique armoire makes a nice bathroom storage cabinet.
- I once leaned an old wooden ladder against my bathroom wall. It held towels and added a bit of architectural interest.
- Sconces on either side of the bathroom mirror provide nice lighting.
- Don't store jewelry in the bathroom; keep it in the dressing area of your bedroom instead.
- Keep your makeup collection simple and store it in a makeup bag or in covered clear plastic shoeboxes that are stackable.

Family Bathroom Etiquette

If your home has only one (or two) small bathrooms but you have several family members, it's critical to the organization of the bathroom—and to family harmony—to keep your bathroom(s) tidy and efficient. Call a family powwow and discuss appropriate bathroom etiquette so that each person's privacy and cleanliness needs are respected.

Some topics and ideas to discuss:

- In the morning when the household is hectic and everyone's getting ready to head out the door, it's stressful if two family members are arguing for bathroom time. Avoid this by assigning a regular time slot for each person to use the shower and vanity each morning. That way everyone knows what to expect and no one is late.

- Likewise, in the evening limit bubble bath soaks and showers to no more than a half hour per family member and assign a time slot.
- No wet towels are permitted on the bathroom floor or vanity. All towels are to be hung up, and once children are old enough, they are responsible for laundering their own towels.
- No dirty clothes are permitted on the bathroom floor.
- Keep a notepad and pen in the vanity drawer so that when someone uses the last of a toiletry, they write it down for the next shopping trip.
- No teenage lotions, potions, and hair products are permitted all over the bathroom. Instead, each person keeps their items in a plastic caddy in their bedroom.
- Each family member is responsible for keeping their own medicine cabinet shelf organized and clean.
- All children's bathtub toys are put away when not in use.
- A package of wet wipes is stored in the vanity, and each family member is responsible for wiping down the countertop and sink when they are done using them.
- Each family member can be assigned a different bathroom cleaning day to clean the toilet, shower, vanity, and mirror when it's their turn.

- Whoever uses the last toilet paper square replaces the roll.
- If you have a glass shower door, each person who showers uses a squeegee to dry the door.
- Dad and sons shall not leave the toilet seat up.
- Mom and daughters shall dispose of feminine products in a sanitary, courteous, ladylike way.
- When someone has the bathroom door locked, they want privacy. Respect it.

Bathroom Style File

As you declutter and organize your bathroom, remember to personalize it for comfort. Add some nice silk plants, and put a pretty bowl with beautiful milled soaps of different colors next to your tub. Mount a small TV on the wall above the tub, and put a CD player on top of a shelf so you can listen to soothing music while getting ready for work. I took a large colorful planter that ordinarily would be used in a garden and had a round piece of glass cut for the top. I used it as an accent table and had it next to my bathtub with romantic candles flickering on it.

And here's a dollar-wise trick for a decorative bathroom shower curtain that will make your room seem larger. Buy a king-size sheet in a color and pattern you like. Wash and iron it, then open up the hem a bit on each end to make a pocket that your shower rod can go through. A king-size sheet is long enough to go from ceiling to floor if you have nine-foot ceilings, and because it goes all the way to the ceiling it makes the tiny bathroom space look bigger by drawing the eye upward. I once used a pale-blue sheet with wavy lines to mimic the ocean waves in a teeny bathroom, and it added a fun twist to the rest of my seaside cottage décor.

Mini-Spa Summary

So there you have it . . . you're on your way to an organized small bathroom that you and your family will love, better known as your mini-spa.

Resources for Small Bathrooms

Baker's Racks
www.HomeDecorators.com
www.HomeGoods.com
www.Target.com

Bath Vanity Sconces
www.BathVanitySconce.com
www.LampsPlus.com

CD/DVD Stands and Shelves
www.ContainerStore.com
www.HomeDecorators.com
www.RacksandStands.com

Decorative Wall Hooks
www.HomeDepot.com
www.Target.com
www.WalMart.com

Glass Shelves
www.HomeDepot.com

Hanging Mesh Toy Bags
www.Amazon.com
www.ContainerStore.com

Nontoxic, No-VOC Paint
www.BenjaminMoore.com
www.BioshieldPaint.com
www.Sherwin-Williams.com

Over-the-Door Shoe Holders
www.ContainerStore.com
www.SpaceSavers.com
www.Target.com

Over-the-Faucet Shower Toiletry Holders
www.ContainerStore.com
www.HomeGoods.com
www.Target.com

Over-the-Toilet Cabinets
www.HomeDecorators.com
www.HomeGoods.com
www.Target.com

Plastic Shoeboxes with Lids
www.ContainerStore.com
www.ShopGetOrganized.com
www.SpaceSavers.com

Plastic Turntables
www.ContainerStore.com
www.Target.com
www.WalMart.com

Pump Soap Dispensers
www.HomeGoods.com
www.Target.com
www.WalMart.com

Silverware Trays
www.ContainerStore.com
www.Target.com
www.WalMart.com

Step Stools
www.Target.com
www.WalMart.com

Wall-Mounted Soap Dispensers
www.Amazon.com
www.FaucetDirect.com

Wicker Baskets
www.Michaels.com
www.Target.com
www.WalMart.com

Wire Roller Carts
www.Target.com
www.WalMart.com

———— YOUR SMALL SPACE NOTES ————

9

Home Office Heaven

How to Organize Your Office for Success

In 1992 when I started Organized With Ease, my hands-on professional organizing company, I specialized in organizing offices. During that time I consulted with many clients, from executives working in big fancy corporate offices to solo entrepreneurs who worked from home, and if there is one thing I learned it's this: *make your home office space a personal reflection of you, and be glad that you are able to work from home.*

Of course, it's paramount that a home office be functional and organized so you can be the most productive. But unless you also personalize the space to make it a pleasant reflection of your personality and work style, you just won't want to spend much time there, especially because working from home is filled with distractions that don't happen in a regular office.

Getting Started

Before you buy a desk, a chair, or anything else for your home office, you'll want to assess your particular working needs by asking yourself these questions:

1. Is my home office space one that will be used as a family/household management center, for my career, or both?
2. Where in my home might I carve out a space that will be quiet yet convenient to other household amenities and family members when needed?
3. Will I be sharing the space with my spouse or other family members?
4. What are my storage needs for supplies and special equipment?
5. How do I find out about neighborhood zoning laws and business permits?
6. Will clients be coming to my home office? If so, do my neighborhood zoning laws permit this?
7. Is there adequate power for computer and office equipment and also proper phone hookups?
8. Do I mind having my home office space out in the open—say, in a corner of the living or dining room—or will that be too noisy for me?
9. Do I have an entire room I can use as a home office, or do I need to find a nook in our home somewhere?
10. Is there adequate overhead and task lighting?
11. Is there room for filing and storage?

12. What type of desk, chair, and office equipment feel most comfortable and appropriate for me?

13. Do I need space for books, resource binders, or other materials?

Notebook Nirvana

As I've mentioned elsewhere in this book, I'm a big advocate of the notebook method to stay organized when you're taking on any project. So as you're planning your home office, once again I suggest you buy a three-ring binder and use it to record your notes and drawings. Put clear page protectors in it so that when you're out shopping you can drop any business cards or receipts in there.

Space Grace

Choosing a space for a home office doesn't have to be daunting, even if you live in a studio apartment. The key is to think outside the box and be flexible as you tour your home to find the best spot. While doing so, keep in mind what type of work you do and/or how your family lives, and choose your space accordingly.

For example, as a professional writer with no children (but one husband who does interrupt me at times!), I need a quiet space in order to produce my best work and to conduct private phone calls with my clients. Even though I share a home office with my hubby and have my own desk where I do the administrative work related to my writing, the other half of my home office where I do my actual consultations is my king-size bed, which works well for me. In contrast, a professional musician may have to soundproof the garage to spare the rest of the family the noise while he composes his next hit song, or an architect may need room to store blueprints. So be sure to take into consideration your and your family's personal needs when choosing and setting up a home office space.

Nifty Nook versus One Whole Room

Most of us who live in small spaces don't have the luxury of turning one whole room into our private home office. Instead we have to choose a space that can do double duty, share a room with another family member, or adapt a small corner or nook. Be open-minded, get creative, and you'll find a space in your home that will work.

Possible Home Office Spaces

- A landing at the top of a stairway may be large enough to house a desk, chair, laptop computer, and filing cabinet. A small office armoire may fit here, too.
- The open space under a stairway, if it's tall enough, may work as a family and household management center.
- Place an office armoire in a corner of your bedroom, living room, dining room, or guest room.
- If your kitchen is large enough, put an office armoire in the corner as your family and household management center.

- The dining room table is always an option, as long as you have a nearby cupboard where you can house all your supplies when you need the table for dinner.
- A small desk and chair in the corner of your living room can be hidden with a decorative folding screen.
- Lofts overlooking living or dining areas make wonderful home offices.
- If your small house has an attic, that's an option.
- A walk-in closet works great as a small home office, and many standard closets with bifold doors will hold two filing cabinets with a board or door on top to create a great desk.
- Make your home office portable by using a laptop computer, cell phone, and portable filing bins with lids. You can store everything in one corner of the room and take it wherever you wish to work, inside or out.
- If you're lucky enough to have a small shed in your backyard, you can turn that into a home office provided you're willing to go to the expense of installing electricity and insulation.

Furniture, Equipment, and Supplies

Once you've decided where you think you'd like to pitch your home office camp, it's time to make a list in your notebook of what you'll need for furniture, equipment, and office supplies. Once you have an idea of what you'll need, also sketch out a furniture arrangement that feels comfortable for you. It doesn't need to be fancy, but be sure to measure your furnishings and equipment. By drawing out a plan, you can move things around on paper until you get the arrangement you want—*before* having to move heavy furniture around! You can also buy furniture templates to draw out your arrangement. See the resources at the end of this chapter.

In general, it works best to put the furniture in a home office against the wall, especially if you are sharing a room with another family member. But that's not always the case. It works well for Steve and me to each take a wall on opposite ends of the room. But another couple I know loves having their desks facing each other so they can converse easily because they work together on projects. Play with the arrangement on paper first until you find what works best for your situation.

Delicious Desk and Chair

Can a desk really be delicious? you ask. *Oh yes!* And I think you should choose one that's oh-so-you. Mine is an Old World carved style with beautiful French legs and gold leaf. I found it in a secondhand/antique store, and I consider it absolutely delicious! Be sure to also choose a chair that's ergonomically fitted to your particular body, is comfortable for you, and that you like. I recently had my ugly black office chair (which happens to be very comfortable) slipcovered so it goes nicely with my desk, and I love spending time there. My hubby, on the other hand, prefers his masculine dark wood office armoire and big black office chair that fits his football-player-size body comfortably. Again, choose the desk and chair style that feels best for *you* and fits your space and body properly.

Home Office Equipment

When it comes to home office equipment, choose a computer, printer, phone, and fax that feel comfortable and are easy for you to use. For instance, I still chuckle to remember the young computer salesman who insisted that it was foolish for me to spend extra money buying a pink laptop computer to match my pink cell phone. I informed him with a smile that if you're both creative *and* organized like I am, and you also work in the design field like I do, that the color of your office equipment does indeed affect one's productivity, and yes, I definitely wanted to buy a *pink* computer! Again, choose wisely and buy the office equipment that you feel most comfortable with.

All-in-One Machines

There are many styles and models of office equipment to choose from, but one thing I do recommend buying are the all-in-one machines. By that I mean those that are a printer, fax machine, copier, and scanner all in one. They pack a big productivity punch while taking up just a little bit of space, and they are inexpensive considering all the functions they perform.

A special note: It's efficient to research and compare prices online. However, before you make your final purchase, I still recommend going to a store to get the added in-person scoop from their trained staff. They can often tell you little tidbits you wouldn't know about when researching online. Once you have all the facts, then you can decide where you want to actually purchase your office equipment.

Power and Cords, Oh My!

As you evaluate where you'll set up your home office, be sure to note whether the room or area has adequate power supply for your computer, printer, cell phone recharger, task lighting, and other gadgets. It never fails that when I move into a new space, from a design perspective I intuitively want to put the computer or TV on the wall that has no outlets. (Luckily, my hubby is good at running power cords around a room under the baseboard!) Be sure to check ahead of time and plan accordingly. And speaking of power cords, they can make your home office look very messy, so check the resources listed below for a handy solution to covering up those ugly (but necessary) equipment cords.

Lighting Love

Also be sure your room has adequate lighting. I prefer floor lamps rather than ceiling fixtures for general lighting, and swing-arm task lighting over my desk so I can move the lamp around, depending on the project. Office armoires and some desks have task lighting built in.

Beautiful Office Supplies

What, you ask, *beautiful office supplies*?! Yes, they are available but sometimes you just have to shop a little longer to find them. Again, choose office supplies that will enhance your productivity and make you want to do your work. If you love color, why not buy purple file folders and colored paper clips? (Although be aware that colored file folders often go out of vogue and then go out of stock.) My own home office supplies, for example, include green polka-dotted binder clips, a beautiful peach floral clipboard, brightly colored index cards for notes, floral notepads, hot-pink mailing envelopes, and of course, my favorite hot-pink roller ball pens! The point is, whatever *your* taste, you can find it these days in office supplies—so why not integrate them into your home office to make it more *fun*?

Office Equipment and Supply List

To make it easy for you to shop, I've included a list of office equipment and supplies on pages 271–74. Like a grocery list, feel free to photocopy it and take it along to your office supply store to make your shopping easier.

Oh, the Paperwork!

I have a theory that in heaven there will be no paperwork! But alas, until we enter the pearly gates, there's plenty of it proliferating every day in our lives, so we may as well deal with it in an organized manner.

Whether you have a career home office or a home management office, paperwork can be placed into four basic categories:

1. In Progress/Take Action
2. Current Files/Action Taken
3. Archive Files
4. Resource Files

I can't emphasize enough to keep your paperwork management system *simple*. And before setting up your system, also ask yourself how paperless you can make your office—perhaps you don't need to print out as much as you are now and instead can keep files on your computer, alleviating excess filing and too many papers. Of course, be sure to have a computer data backup plan.

In Progress Paperwork

"In Progress" papers are those that you need to take some kind of action on. For these, I suggest setting up what I call WIP (Work In Progress) files, which is easy to do. Here's how:

Buy:
- A portable file bin that holds hanging files
- Hanging file folders with plastic tabs for labels
- Interior manila file folders
- A label maker or bold black pen to write labels

Label your file tabs with whatever terms make sense to you, and arrange them in alphabetical order so that you can find the information you need when you need it. Put a label on both the hanging file *and* the interior file so that when you remove an interior file you know where to put it back.

Examples of labels:
- To Do
- To Pay
- To Call
- To Read
- Waiting to Hear

Remember that these papers eventually need action, so don't leave them in these files too long. Your WIP files are only for sorting the papers as you process them.

Current/Action Taken Files

You'll also need a set of files for once you've taken action on the papers in your WIP files but you don't want to get rid of the paper just yet. Set up another portable filing bin with a lid, or use a filing cabinet drawer. Again, use hanging files and label the files in a way that makes sense to you, in alphabetical order.

Examples:

- Automobile Maintenance
- Health Insurance Claims (and the year)
- John's School Permission Forms

Once a paper no longer needs to be in your WIP file because action on it is complete, either toss it if you don't need to keep it, or file it here. Once a year, go through and toss anything you don't need in your Current Files/Action Taken, or move it to your Archive files.

Archive Files

Again, set up your Archive files alphabetically in a portable plastic lidded bin with hanging file folders and tabs, or in a filing drawer. File anything in there that you need to keep longer than the current year. Taxes and business files would fall into this category, for instance. Plastic bins with lids work well for Archive files because they stack and store easily in a closet and you can quickly pull a bin out into your home office if you need it. Label each bin by year and topic on the outside, and go through your Archive files once a year to make sure you still need them. If you are in doubt about which files to keep in your Archive files and how long to keep them, hire a professional organizer who specializes in filing systems and/or contact your accountant and tax attorney for the most current information.

Resource Files

Resource files are just that: resources you need to do your work or manage your household. For example, research you've done on purchasing a new bed, possible publishers for the book you're going to write, or articles related to a project you're working on. Set up your Resource files just like I've already mentioned. You can also put your resource materials in three-ring binders, or use a combination of both files and binders like I do.

One Last Filing Note

After years of organizing office after office with clients, and after setting up new offices when I've changed residences, I still recommend a simple A to Z alphabetical filing system. Label the folders the way they make sense to *you*, since every family's file names are different. Remember *KISS: Keep It Super Simple!*

Mail Mountains

Where does most of the paper that comes into your home and office come from anyway? Why, the mail, of course!

Again, to keep paperwork simple, get off as many mailing lists as you can, especially catalog lists since you can find so much information online these days. Also, when my husband and I rented a Postal Annex box I was amazed to find that they sorted out the junk mail flyers for us, substantially limiting the amount of paperwork that came into our home office. I love using their facility and services.

Mail Processing

In order to keep the onslaught of paperwork under control, mail needs to be processed daily.

Here's how:

- Buy a letter opener and keep it on your home office desk.
- Have a stapler and paperclips at hand.
- Slit open each envelope. If you don't need the return address, immediately shred and/or recycle the envelope and any extraneous ads or paper you don't need.
- Clip the papers to any return envelope.
- File the paper in the proper action WIP file—for example, To Pay, To Read, Invitations—and act on it later.
- Add any upcoming events to your calendar.

Be sure not to let your mail pile up inside your WIP files. Again, those files are just a holding place for sorting until you can take the time to process the papers.

Emergency Files

Since most of us encounter some kind of natural disaster at some time in our lives (I live in earthquake territory . . . need I say more?), setting up a portable emergency file is very wise. Again, simply purchase a portable plastic filing bin with a lid and some hanging file folders with plastic labels. File your insurance policies, birth certificates, passports, and other important papers in there so you can simply grab and go should an emergency arise.

If you feel more comfortable filing the original documents in your safe or safety deposit box, make photocopies of them for your emergency evacuation box because having the copies with policy and phone numbers on them will be helpful should you need them. I can tell you from personal experience that after evacuating for a week during the California wildfires, we were so glad our emergency file box was ready to take with us.

Phone Message Paper

Whether you have a land line, a cell phone, or a combination of both, it's good to record your phone messages, and there are several easy ways to do so. I personally like a spiral-bound, preprinted phone message book with carbons so I have a copy, but others prefer just a plain small spiral-bound notebook where they can record calls. A small notebook works great to store in your purse or briefcase and use with your cell phone. Some people also like the printed pink phone message pads that tear off at the top. You can get any of these at the office supply store. The important thing is to write down your phone messages and to train your children how to take phone messages as well. Once the call has been returned or the task related to the call is completed (e.g., buy bread), recycle the paper.

Going Green

Remember to recycle as much paper as possible in your home office. Using a shredder helps compact it, as well as protecting your privacy.

Some printer cartridges can be recycled; others can't. It's wise green living to inquire about this when you purchase a new printer. Search online to find places that might take your particular cartridges and recycle them.

Outdated office equipment such as computers, cell phones, and copiers can sometimes be donated or recycled. Google your particular piece of equipment along with your city for current information.

Art Smart

Now that you've set up your small home office space in a productive and comfortable way, once again it's time to treat yourself! Art is a nice way to do so and will further personalize your space. Maybe you'd like to have family pictures on your office walls. You could have your crowning achievements framed and on display. Or perhaps a photo from your favorite family vacation to Fiji enlarged to poster size is more your style. Again, choose something for your walls that will be oh-so-you.

Resources for Small Home Offices

Furniture Layout Templates
www.DecoratorTrainingInstitute
.com

Office Armoires
www.BallardDesigns.com
www.HomeDecorators.com

Office Equipment and Supplies
www.OfficeDepot.com
www.OfficeMax.com
www.Staples.com

Office Equipment and Supplies Checklist
See pages 271–74.

Office Equipment Cord Control
www.CableCordOrganizer.com

Office Furniture (that doesn't feel like office furniture)
www.BallardDesigns.com
www.EthanAllen.com
www.HomeDecorators.com
www.WestElm.com

—— YOUR SMALL SPACE NOTES ——

10

Mastering Your Small Master Bedroom, Bath, and Closet

No matter the size of the room, is there any place in your home more personal than the master bedroom and bath suite? It's where we rest when we're weary, lovingly entwine our hearts, bodies, and souls in marriage, snuggle our babies, bathe our cares away, and cuddle down to watch a movie with a big bowl of popcorn, to name just a few of life's precious moments that take place there.

Sacred Space

As an organizer, decorator, and a wife of over thirty years, I'm a firm believer that the master suite is the most special and sacred area in our homes and that no matter how small it is, you *deserve* yours to be a beautiful and nurturing haven.

It's worth your time, effort, and money to make it so. After all, it's the place where you wake up *every morning* to start your day, and the condition and ambience of this room set the tone for how the rest of your day will go.

Getting Started

While all bedrooms share certain organizing needs, the master bedroom suite deserves your special organizational attention since it is your most personal space. And although this book focuses on home organizing and not interior decorating, I would like you to be thinking of how you'd like your room to ultimately feel.

We'll begin here, as in every room, with a three-ring binder and dreaming a plan of action before you ever begin any physical work. So before you roll up those sleeves to start organizing your new master suite, pour yourself a cup of coffee or tea, grab your notebook, and dream and doodle!

Intimate versus Small

Since your room is small, aim for creating an intimate feeling of serenity. Begin the process by recalling the most lovely bedrooms or suites you've ever stayed in while on vacation or when you were a guest in someone's home. Perhaps you've stayed in an elegant hotel room or a cozy beach cottage that you fondly remember. Was there a room that absolutely spoke to your heart and soul that you'd like to re-create?

Honeymoon Haven

What was your honeymoon room or suite like? If you loved it, then why not re-create it at home? (And if you didn't love it, consider it your education in what *not* to do!) As a writer for wedding magazines who interviews many brides, I've learned that it's cost-effective, not to mention sentimental, to use items and colors from your wedding in your master bedroom suite. One mother of the bride sewed beautiful cushions for her daughter's wedding reception sofas, which the couple then used as part of their new master bedroom décor. Another couple used the silk floral arrangements from their wedding in their boudoir. Yet another bride and groom framed their wedding photo in a large ornate frame, had their wedding guests sign the matting that surrounded the photo, and hung it above their bed.

Before we explore my organizing ideas, tap into your own personal experiences and memories so you can make your master bedroom *your* perfect retreat.

Real-Life Examples

Beachy Retreat

When my friend's husband was diagnosed with a difficult illness, she told me tearfully that she was tired of their disorderly master bedroom and bathroom and that she was especially weary of her messy dresser. She wanted to redo their bedroom as a gift to her husband. I heartily agreed and offered to help her virtually from across the country. I suggested that together we come up with a plan to turn their suite into a seaside retreat, reminiscent of the time we all spent together a year earlier having a delicious lunch over-looking the ocean in beautiful California.

My friend's voice lit up on the phone as I gave her suggestions for organizing her dresser as well as ideas for paint and bedding colors to evoke a calm seaside feeling. I also suggested she remove the old closet doors that were falling off their hinges, customize the closet with shelving to better organize their clothes, and hang beautiful sand-colored curtains where the closet doors once were.

Soon . . . *presto*! She was excitedly calling me, telling me she had found the perfect beach-themed art and just the right color comforter and matching bathroom towels. Before long, her husband came home to his new orderly "seaside oasis" where he could rest and regroup from his medical treatments, and she said he absolutely loved the room.

Tropical Retreat

One of my hands-on organizing clients loved to travel to tropical locales. After we organized and downsized her two-bedroom condo into a much smaller one-bedroom condo in an elegant new building that better fit her current lifestyle, she began asking me for ideas on how to make her one bedroom/bathroom into a breezy master suite with a tropical feel. I suggested keeping it casually elegant and ethereal because that's how she lived and even dressed; that was "her."

Since she loved to travel to Florida beaches and wanted to re-create a carefree tropical theme, her tiny master bedroom and bath indeed soon became a soothing oasis. She shirred and draped sheer fabric along the walls to create the feeling of mosquito nets. She bought colorful bed linens with a tropical flair to cover her gorgeous antique bed, and her small adjacent bathroom soon boasted new plush towels, wicker baskets stocked with small toiletries, and a palm plant. Finally, she added a beautiful orchid, turning her ordinary little bathroom into a serene "seaside spa" for very little money.

Bed-and-Breakfast Retreat

My husband and I are big bed-and-breakfast inn travelers. We've stayed in over sixty inns in seventeen states since 1987, and I've taken photos of all those inns and put them in scrapbooks.

Whenever we organize and redecorate our master bedroom we refer to our inn photo albums to recapture the order and lovely sumptuousness of some of the rooms we have stayed in. I modeled our current all-white bedroom makeover after an exquisite room at a Palm Springs inn where we stayed for our thirtieth anniversary. For under $1,000 I created a serene white haven, complete with a big fluffy down comforter, a pretty ivory swag of fabric hanging over our king-size bed, and oodles of white pillows of different sizes, fabric textures, and designs. I fondly refer to it as "White Haven Lane." (You can see photos on my blog at www.KathrynBechen.com.) Clutter is kept to a minimum because necessities are stored in white or natural wicker baskets of differing shapes and sizes to create decorative interest.

Previously Steve and I created a rose-themed cottage motif in our master bedroom suite, and that room was featured in a national decorating magazine. It really didn't cost much to emulate the look of the B&B bedrooms we stayed in, and you can do that too. The key is to shop at discount stores and buy the best quality goods you can find, *for less.*

Online Idea Factory

If you need more bedroom ideas and sample photos, search my favorite inn site, www.ILoveInns.com, which has photos from beautiful inn bedrooms from all over the world. Another idea is to Google a city you've visited (for instance, "San Francisco lodging" or "New York City lodging") and look at the bedroom photos on the lodging websites. Decorating blogs are another good choice for free photos of real-life bedrooms. Touring model homes in person is another way to get good organizing, storage, and decorating ideas for your own master suite.

Function Junction

As you're planning your new master bedroom's organization, be sure to consider the lifestyle functions you (and your spouse if you have one) personally perform there, because function is critical to your final result. For instance, some people *only* sleep in their bedrooms and don't watch TV or allow their pets in there. Others allow their pets right in bed with them and have movie and popcorn night in their bedroom every Saturday night. Some families don't mind toys in their master bedroom, and others strictly forbid their kids to play in their master suite. Again, think how *you* actually live and then plan accordingly; many a mom with little children has told me that while she loved seeing my own all-white master bedroom photos, it would never work in her home because of her kids' chocolate-covered hands and her dog's muddy paws! So be sure to create a room that works best for *your* lifestyle.

Questions to Consider

As you're planning your new master bedroom suite, below are some questions to ask yourself:

- Do we like and still need all the furniture in our master bedroom? If not, what do we need to replace or remove?
- Do we like to watch TV in our bedroom, or not?
- Will we allow our kids to play with their toys in our master bedroom, or is it off-limits to our children? If their toys are allowed, is there storage for them?
- Will our pets be allowed, and if so, on the bed? Is there a pet blanket for the bed?
- Do we like to eat and drink in bed, or is food strictly off-limits?
- Do we want a mini-refrigerator and a cupboard for snacks?
- Do we want to do any work in our bedroom? If so, how are we going to hide it when we're not working? Do we need a desk and chair or a laptop and lap desk?
- Do we read in our bedroom? If so, do we read in bed or do we have room for an easy chair and lamp?
- Is our lighting adequate?
- Do we work on hobbies in our master bedroom? If so, do we have the proper supplies and a way to conceal them when not in use to avoid a cluttered look?
- Is our storage adequate?

- Do we need an air purifier or white noise machine to help us sleep?
- Is our closet doing its job in keeping our wardrobe organized properly? If not, what can we change?
- Is our master bathroom orderly and functional already? If not, what can we change and what do we need to improve?
- Do we have a basket or hamper for dirty laundry, and do we want it kept in the bedroom, the bathroom, or the laundry room?
- Do my mate and I agree on what constitutes a serene and orderly master suite? If not, what can we do to compromise?

Decluttering Time

Waking up to a cluttered room full of dirty laundry, junk on your dressers, and piles of old magazines does not start your day out on a positive note. So you'll first want to declutter your room and possibly rearrange your furnishings, knick-knacks, and art.

Here's how.

Bedroom Bliss

Gather three large drawstring trash bags and label them Donate, Toss, and Sell/Consign. Walk around your bedroom and put anything you no longer need or want in the proper bag. Check every nook, cranny, and surface and get rid of as many old magazines, books, and knickknacks as you can. You should also donate outdated artwork hanging on your walls that will not contribute to your new look. Remember, since it's your master suite and your haven of serenity, be ruthless about getting rid of anything that doesn't contribute to a feeling of calm.

Clean Living

Once you've removed anything you no longer want or need, clean your bedroom thoroughly. Dust and vacuum, wash the bedding, wash or dry-clean the curtains, and steam-clean the carpet. If you need new bed linens and window treatments, make a note to purchase them, but at least your current ones will be clean until you can shop for new ones. And speaking of clean, I suggest you keep your laundry hamper in your master bedroom closet. Be sure to buy an attractive one that goes with your décor.

Furniture Arrangement

Once you've decluttered your bedroom, take a look at your furnishings and accessories. Are you happy with their arrangement? It's always wise to draw out your furniture arrangement on paper before actually moving it. Also, you can purchase furniture layout templates to make the job on paper even easier. Check the resources section at the end of this chapter.

Oh to Bed

A special note here about your bed. Choose a style and size that is most comfortable for you and your mate and then make it the most sumptuous and sensuous nest you can by dressing it in soft linens that soothingly kiss your skin for ultimate comfort. You can find wonderful quality linens at discount stores like Marshalls, Home Goods, and T J Maxx. Choose sheets with a 400 thread count or higher.

Going Green

Organic beds are now available, as are luxuriously soft organic linens (see the resources section at the end of this chapter). If you can't afford organic linens, soak brand-new regular linens overnight in your washing machine in a mixture of vinegar, baking soda, and water, and then wash them a couple of times the next day with nontoxic laundry detergent. This helps remove the "no ironing needed" chemicals that can trigger allergies.

More Bed Bliss

Ordinarily it works best to place the head of your bed along the longest wall, or you can angle it in a corner or even put it in front of a window. Also, you don't have to have a headboard; I opted to hang a painting over my bed along with the fabric swag I mentioned earlier. Get creative! I've also hung an old piece of architectural salvage over my bed as an interesting "headboard." (Be careful to mount anything over the bed very securely; you don't want it falling on you!)

Nightstands or Not

Most people like nightstands next to the bed with drawers to hold tissues, a flashlight, and other nighttime necessities. But if you're a "moderne" minimalist, perhaps a sleek chrome table would suit you better. If you read in bed, a bookcase tower on either side of your bed with baskets on some of the shelves to hold tissues and such may be the preferred option for you.

More Storage

If you have room, a rectangular ottoman with a hinged lid works great at the end of your bed for storing extra linens. You can also use under-the-bed plastic lidded roller bins for seasonal clothing. Armoires work great for housing your TV and media equipment because they can be closed when not in use.

Creature Comforts

Once you've decluttered your bedroom and arranged your furniture the way you want it, remember to place your creature comforts and other accessories in an artful way. The organizing details are what make a house feel like a home, so don't skip this step. (But please don't get carried away with too many knickknacks, either.) Use personal items that speak to your heart; framed photos of your kids, your pets, and your travels are good choices.

To personalize my own master suite I have topiary plants in antique containers, some pretty framed photos of our beloved kitties, two bookcases of my favorite inspirational/comfort books, and a beautiful pastel painting that was a gift to me from a former organizing client. I also created a "happy wall" of framed photos of my husband and me sharing fun experiences. It makes me smile every time I walk by! Personalize *your* suite!

Master Closet Cleverness

An important part of your master suite is your closet, be-cause if it's not organized, clothes and other stuff will likely overflow into your bedroom, causing clutter and chaos. Whether or not you have a small walk-in closet, two side closets, or just one small closet in your master suite, you can make it work well for you. The key is to always think of your closet as a little "boutique." Unlike department stores, only items that are the cream of the crop make it into fancy boutiques. With that in mind, let's start decluttering your closet.

Divide and Conquer

Since you're going to start thinking of your closet as a boutique from now on, get rid of anything that no longer fits or is out of style. (Like your 1966 prom dress or that embroidered jean jacket you wore in college!) Trust me, you're never going to wear some of those things again, so be *ruthless*! Label trash bags as Donate, Consign, Garage Sale, and so forth. Then sort your items into them and out they go.

Going Green

Try to *never* throw clothing in the trash (where it will end up in landfills) unless it's totally full of holes and unwearable. Even then, quilters may be able to use the fabric to make quilts. Instead, donate used clothing to your local charity, consign it to your favorite consignment store, or give it to family and friends.

Closet Evaluation

Take everything out of your closet and then take a look at the closet. No matter the size, it's always best to have at least some double-hung shelving instead of only one rod because you can hang more clothes that way. So add another rod if you need to do so. Also hang a shelf above the top rod for storing extra clothing or shoes. Another option is to buy Elfa shelving and rods and customize the system to your closet. See the resources section.

Mate Harmony

If you share a closet with your mate, you should each take one side if it's a walk-in closet, or one end if it's a long closet with sliding doors. If you have just one tiny closet *and* a mate, in the interest of marital harmony I suggest buying a portable wardrobe or armoire so that each partner has their own closet space.

Clothes Categorizing

Once your closet has the proper rods and shelves, separate your clothes into categories: slacks, tops, dresses, suits, and so forth. Count how many items you have and purchase enough of the right hangers for each type of garment (e.g., suit hangers, slack hangers, dress and top hangers). I like either clear hard plastic hangers with a swivel hook on top or slimline velveteen hangers.

Hang like items together and further organize each category by color. That makes it easy to get dressed in the morning and you look "put together" because you can see at a glance exactly what's available.

Clever Closet Organizing Tip

To keep her closet under control, one friend told me that when she buys a new piece of clothing, out goes an old one. That's because she purposely keeps only so many hangers as a "signal" to herself that her closet is already full enough.

Shoe Savvy

Hanging an over-the-door shoe holder on the back of your swinging closet door works well for women's shoes, but I've found that the pockets are sometimes too small for men's shoes. Be sure to take note of that when you purchase one. You might do better to purchase the style of shoe holder that hangs on the closet rod rather than over the door. Also, if you have a lot of shoes and only one door to your closet, it's fine to put one mate's shoes in the master bedroom closet and the other's in a hall closet. Another option would be to store one partner's shoes in plastic lidded roller bins under the bed.

Storage Delights

Plastic stacking drawers work great inside a walk-in closet to store your socks, undies, and workout wear. My hubby and I have twelve small stacking drawers for this purpose, and we love it because we can see everything at a glance since the drawers are clear. These types of storage drawers are also an affordable alternative to a chest of drawers.

Clever Containers

Since your master closet is a boutique (remember?), I'd also encourage you to personalize it with lovely storage containers. Places like Home Goods and T J Maxx sell beautiful stacking paper boxes in a variety of colors and designs. Round hatboxes add beauty *and* work great for storage, as do wicker baskets with fabric liners. I have a floral hatbox in my master bedroom walk-in closet that I use to store my extra small purses. Pretty rectangular boxes on my top closet shelf hold greeting cards that my hubby and I have given each other, as well as sentimental letters from friends that I've saved over the years.

Master Bathroom Bliss

Now that you've organized your master bedroom, it's time to talk about the master bathroom. I've already given you many organizing ideas for small bathrooms in chapter 8, so what I'd most like to share with you here is that like your master bedroom, your master bathroom should be highly personalized.

Bubble-icious

Choose shampoos and soaps that feel luxurious to you and store them in a wicker basket by your tub. Add a fragrant floral plant and buy the softest, plushest towels you can find in a yummy color you love. Hang terrycloth robes for you and your mate on the back of the bathroom door. You get the picture—your master bathroom is an extension of your master bedroom and part of your sensuous "suite nest"!

Courteous Mates

If you share the master bathroom with your mate (not everyone does; my hubby prefers to use our other bathroom as his own private getaway spot and lets me have the master bathroom to myself), be courteous about sharing the space. Keep the room clean by picking up after yourself and don't leave pantyhose drying on the towel bar or whiskers in the sink.

One Last Tip

Well, there you have it—you've now created the organized master bedroom and bath of your dreams! Let me leave you with one last organizing tip, one that's so simple but makes such a difference on a daily basis: *make your bed every day.* It's the first thing I do in the morning, right when I get out of bed. Your bed is a large surface in the room, and simply by making it up every day, there'll be an immediate visual sense of order.

Resources for Small Master Bedroom Suites

Armoires
www.BallardDesigns.com
www.EthanAllen.com
www.HomeDecorators.com

Bookcases
www.BallardDesigns.com
www.HomeDecorators.com
www.Ikea.com

Closet Shelving
www.ContainerStore.com
www.Elfa.com
www.Ikea.com

Creating a "Honeymoon Style" Master Bedroom
www.ILoveInns.com
www.MatthewAlexanderCreations.com
www.SanDiegoStyleWeddings.com

Decorative Paper Storage and Hatboxes
www.Marshalls.com
www.TJMaxx.com

Hangers
www.OnlySlimlineHangers.com
www.Target.com
www.WalMart.com

Organic Beds
www.GreenNest.com
www.LifeKind.com
www.PureRest.com

Shoe Storage
www.ContainerStore.com
www.OrganizedAtoZ.com
www.ShopGetOrganized.com

Stacking Plastic Drawers
www.ContainerStore.com
www.ShopGetOrganized.com
www.Target.com

Storage Ottomans
www.BallardDesigns.com
www.HomeDecorators.com

Under-the-Bed Storage Containers
www.ContainerStore.com
www.ShopGetOrganized.com
www.Target.com

———————— YOUR SMALL SPACE NOTES ————————

Bedroom Bliss

Organizing Bedrooms and Guest Rooms

Ah yes, the classic multipurpose bedroom is often a clutter magnet rather than a functional and useful room. So it's time to reclaim your small extra bedroom and make it an orderly and useful room that's perfectly suited to you and your family. Let's get started by brainstorming, and be sure to take notes in your three-ring binder.

Choose a Fun Function or Theme

The first thing you'll want to decide about your extra bedroom is how you want to use it. Since you do live in a small home, your room will likely have to serve several purposes. Here are some suggestions, and you can, of course, mix and match the ideas to do double or triple duty.

Den

I have a friend who lived in a small raised-ranch style tract home of about one thousand square feet. Since their home had a small living room and no family room, she decided that once her daughter became a teenager, it was time to move her to a remodeled basement bedroom and turn her tiny bedroom on the main floor into a family den. Off came the sliding doors to the bedroom's closet, and into the closet opening went a wooden entertainment center unit that housed their TV and board games. They bought a beautiful sleeper sofa to place opposite the closet wall and—voilà! The room was quickly turned into a cozy den, and the sleeper sofa enabled the room to double as a guest room when needed.

Music Room

You say your son has taken up the saxophone and the noise is driving you mad? You might consider lining the walls of the room with foam rubber covered with interesting fabric for soundproofing. Let him practice in there to his heart's content (and your ears' relief!).

Art Studio

If you've been longing to take up painting, why not turn your extra bedroom into a little art studio? I know of an interior designer who turned her recently married daughter's bedroom into an art "gallery" where she displayed and sold paintings they had collected over the years.

Hobby Room

Been hankering to take up quilting or scrapbooking? Line the perimeter of the room with work tables and store supplies underneath the tables and in the closet. If you place a twin trundle bed against one wall your room can double as a guest room.

Playroom

If your kids' toys are strewn all over the house and you're tired of tripping over them, why not create a colorful kids' playroom and insist that all toys be used and stored only in there.

Library

A tiny bedroom makes for a cozy library, and it's easy to create. Line the perimeter of your room with bookcases from floor to ceiling, add a comfy chair and ottoman, bring in a cup of tea, and you're on your way to library love!

Game Room

If you prefer checkers and backgammon to Friday night TV, why not turn your extra bedroom into a family game room complete with a game table and a wide variety of games stored in the closet. Or perhaps a pool table is more your style.

Sewing Room

A friend's mother makes the most exquisite wedding dresses you can imagine, all from her spare bedroom. Another friend's mother made all her beautiful clothes from a tiny bedroom in their home. If you're a seamstress, perhaps you could even turn your sewing hobby into a home business.

Man Cave

Since the dawn of time men have hunkered down in their caves to think and "process," so why not create a man cave for *your* special man. I once turned a bedroom into my hubby's golf cave, and he loved it.

Bed-and-Breakfast Guest Room

If you like to stay in bed-and-breakfast inns like my hubby and I do, why not turn your spare bedroom into a guest room reminiscent of your favorite inn? Your guests will love it, and you can also use it as your own getaway room when you don't have time to travel to an actual inn.

Let's Get Organized

Whether you choose to turn your extra bedroom into a toy room, a library, or a guest room, you'll want to go through several logical steps to assure the final orderly result. Again, draw out your furniture arrangement on paper and make lists in your notebook of what you need to buy and what you can use from other rooms in your home.

Delectable Decluttering

Once you've decided what purpose(s) you want to use your room for, it's time to declutter. Again, set up trash bags labeled *Toss, Donate, Sell, Give to Family*, and so on. Then start getting rid of anything you don't need, or move it to a different place in your home if you want to keep it. If you're changing the entire theme of your room, it's best to remove *everything* from the room so you have a blank canvas to work with and can more easily evaluate your space. Even in a small room, it works best to declutter in two-hour time blocks and then take a break so you don't get overwhelmed. Once you've removed everything from the room, clean it thoroughly, decide if you need to repaint, steam clean the carpet, and dry-clean or wash your window treatments.

A Blank Canvas

Now that you've decided what you want your room's theme and function to be and have decluttered and cleaned it thoroughly, here are some questions to ask yourself before setting up your new space:

1. What are my storage needs for the particular kind of room I am creating?
2. Is the closet sufficient for storage, or will I need to purchase additional storage pieces? If so, what kind?
3. What furniture do I have in other areas of my home that I could move to this room (e.g., a chest of drawers or a game/card table)?
4. Is the flooring adequate for my room's theme? If you're creating a sewing room or art studio, for instance, it might be better to choose a flooring other than carpet.
5. Is there enough lighting in this room for my needs? If not, do I need to purchase lighting, or can I move a lamp from another room? Would a combination ceiling fan/light fixture work best?
6. If I have small items that go with a particular hobby, how and where am I going to store them? Do I want

them in full view at my fingertips or behind closed doors?

7. What furniture do I need to make this room comfortable (e.g., bookcases, chairs, sleeper sofa, card table, storage ottoman)?

8. Will I be the only one using this room, or will other family members and guests also be using it? If so, how often?

9. If I have paperwork that accompanies my hobbies, how will I file it? Do I have the proper filing tools, or do I need to purchase them?

10. Will I have manuals such as notebooks that need to be stored on bookshelves?

11. Do I want to be able to listen to music in this room? If so, how will I do that?

12. Are the electrical and computer connections in this room sufficient, or do I need to add more?

13. What ambience do I want the finished room to have and what decorative elements must I purchase to achieve the feeling I want?

Guest Room Graciousness

If you decide to use your extra bedroom as a guest room—even just part of the time—it's wise to take into account my suggestions below so that both you and your guests are as comfortable as possible. It's ultimately up to you to decide whether your family is even comfortable having overnight guests in your small home. Some families are not; likewise, some people prefer to stay in a hotel or bed-and-breakfast inn rather than at someone's home.

- *Comfortable Bed.* Since your room is small and is likely serving other functions than just a guest room, it's wise to choose a sleeper sofa because it will leave room for other activities in the room. They come in standard and queen sizes, and there are also loveseats that pull out into a twin-size bed. An alternative to a sleeper sofa is a twin bed with a trundle underneath it that pulls out so you can accommodate more than one guest.
- *Lovely Linens.* Be sure to provide your guests with lovely sheets and enough blankets and pillows, especially in the winter. And two sets of fluffy fresh towels are a nice touch.
- *Nifty Nightstand.* You'll want to position the bed so that a nightstand, small table, or bookshelf is nearby where guests can place their alarm clock and personal items.
- *Lemonade Love.* How welcoming to leave a pitcher of lemonade or water and a pretty glass on the nightstand beside the bed!
- *Door Lock.* Make sure your guest room door has a lock to prevent wandering children from seeing Uncle John in his birthday suit.
- *Bathroom Bliss.* Be sure there's bathroom access nearby and provide a wicker or plastic basket guests can use to take their toiletries to the bathroom.

- *Optimized Outlets.* Make sure there's an outlet available for your guests to plug in their cell phone charger and laptop computer.
- *Feisty Fido.* Be considerate of the possibility that your guests may be allergic to your pets or may not be pet lovers. Act accordingly so both of you are comfortable with the situation. It's wise to address this issue before you agree to have a guest stay with you.
- *Magazines and Books.* It's a nice touch to place a basket of magazines and paperback books that you think your guests might like next to their bed.

Super Storage Solutions

Turning your small bedroom into a functional multipurpose or themed room requires some clever storage solutions. Here is a potpourri of my best organizing and storage tips for creating a multipurpose room:

- Remove sliding closet doors and place a wooden entertainment center inside the closet to store craft and office supplies.
- Stackable plastic drawers work great to store craft supplies, copy paper, and office supplies.
- Large glass fishbowls are an attractive way to display colorful skeins of yarn and embroidery thread.
- Look around your home for containers that might work well to store your craft supplies. Hatboxes and antique cups, mugs, and urns are good choices.

- A portable wardrobe with a flat top holds out-of-season clothing and you can store craft or other supplies on top of it.
- Place a door over two nightstands to create a work table, and you can store items in the drawers of the nightstands.
- Baker's racks make interesting and attractive bookcases and craft supply shelves.
- Store extra craft items in stackable plastic bins with lids and hide them behind a folding screen.
- Buy a lap desk and sit on your sofa bed to use your laptop computer rather than sitting at a desk.
- An antique music cabinet works well to store copy paper or folded guest towels.
- Planters work well to hold craft supplies and add a colorful and whimsical touch to the room.
- Photo boxes come in all colors and patterns and are a great tool for stackable storage. I put office supplies in mine and label the front of each box with a label maker.
- Wicker baskets can hold everything from extra sheets to copy paper to the afghan you're knitting.
- Dishpans on bookcases work great for storing kids' toys because they "pull out" just like a drawer and you can label the front of them.
- Use a wicker hamper to attractively house extra linens and blankets in your guest room.
- Choose double-duty furniture like hinged storage ottomans and sleeper sofas.

- Rolling metal tool carts with drawers hold blueprints and large papers well.
- Use under-the-bed plastic storage bins to hold out-of-season clothes, toys, shoes, and hobby supplies.
- Antique furnishings often have little cubbies that work great for storing small items.
- Use a trunk as a coffee table and to store blankets and pillows.
- Two-drawer filing cabinets can be placed all along one wall to use as storage for craft supplies.
- Laundry baskets work great for holding kids' small toys.
- Pottery Barn makes a wonderful platform bed with the choice of either pull-out drawers or wicker baskets below the mattress for storage; it's called the Stratton bed.

Organizing Wrap-Up

Now that you've made your spare bedroom into the perfect all-purpose or theme room you've been dreaming of, I'm confident you're going to love spending time there as much as I enjoyed the den I created in one small house we lived in. My room was so cozy I never wanted to leave! I had a carpenter install French doors that I found at an antique store, I stored my journals in an antique trunk that had been decoupaged with beautiful floral wallpaper, and I bought a comfy floral chintz wicker loveseat. A reproduction Queen Anne style desk completed the room, and I was in heaven. May you find this kind of bliss in *your* room!

Resources for Small Multipurpose Bedrooms

Baker's Racks
www.BakersRacks.com
www.EthanAllen.com
www.HomeDecorators.com

Elfa Custom Closet Organizers/ Shelves
www.ContainerStore.com
www.Elfa.com

Lap Desks
www.BarnesandNoble.com
www.Levenger.com

Rolling Metal Tool Carts
www.AutoAnything.com
www.Sears.com
www.Target.com

Sleeper Sofas
www.EthanAllen.com
www.FlexSteel.com

Stackable Plastic Storage Drawers and Bins
www.ContainerStore.com
www.ShopGetOrganized.com
www.Target.com

Storage Ottomans
www.BallardDesigns.com
www.EthanAllen.com

Stratton Storage Bed
www.PotteryBarn.com

Trunks
www.Pier1.com

Under-the-Bed Storage
www.ContainerStore.com
www.OrganizedAtoZ.com
www.ShopGetOrganized.com

Wicker Hampers
www.BathroomFurnitureDirect.com
www.HomeDecorators.com
www.HomeGoods.com

----- YOUR SMALL SPACE NOTES -----

_____

_____

_____

_____

_____

_____

_____

_____

_____

_____

_____

_____

_____

_____

_____

_____

_____

_____

_____

12

And Baby Makes Three

Setting Up a Nursery in a Small Home

Although Steve and I don't have children, my experience with kids ranges from babysitting during my teenage years, to working as a live-in nanny, to being certified as a school teacher/tutor. I've also been an observant friend to many mothers of all ages who have graciously invited me into their lives and homes over the years. If there's one thing I'm absolutely certain of, it's this: when a baby is born, the organizational landscape of both the couple *and* the home undergoes dramatic change, *especially* if the family lives in a small space.

I'm also a firm believer that no matter how small the home a child is raised in, kids both need and deserve to have a room that fosters their maximum personal growth—physically, intellectually, and emotionally. It all starts with the nursery, and my observation is that parents who plan their baby's room well in advance of the birth and work on it together as a couple or family seem to have an easier transition with all the stuff that goes along with having a baby—from clothes, to diapers, to bottles, to strollers. Why not make it easy and fun for the whole family by being prepared?

As we get started on organizing your child's nursery, right off the bat I'll tell you my all-time best advice for a baby's first space: hug and kiss your sweet little one, and also *KISS* their nursery! By *KISS* the nursery I mean "Keep It Super Simple." And as you're creating the room, always keep in mind that your child's safety is paramount. (For that matter, be sure the rest of your home is safe for your children too, not just the nursery.)

KISS Nursery Example

With all the baby shower, friend, and grandma gifts your new little bundle of joy is likely to receive, is it *really* possible to *KISS* your baby's nursery? *Yes!* Does that mean it has to be dull and drab? *No!* It's simply a matter of making smart choices, as the following real-life stories clearly show.

Many years ago, I adventurously left the rural plains of the Midwest as a starry-eyed eighteen-year-old college girl, and I boarded a plane to exciting New York City to work as a live-in nanny for a summer. My first impression of the home in which I would be living was that the sweet toddler I took care of was indeed fortunate because her nursery was colorful, clutter-free, and soothing for a child's spirit. (Not to mention their entire home was the most clutter-free home I think I have ever seen!)

I loved spending time in that sweet nursery with my young charge. The fresh white modern crib had a colorful mobile hanging over it, and there was a changing table with a matching chest of drawers. A small closet held just a few cute outfits and a couple pair of shoes in her current size. Big windows let in sunshine, the carpet was bright blue, and red wooden letters spelling her name charmingly hung over the changing table. Toys were well chosen but minimal and were stored in a laundry basket when not being used.

Contrast that cheerful and streamlined nursery with a nursery belonging to an acquaintance of mine who was a shopaholic. Her baby's closet was stuffed with so many clothes, toys, and shoes that the door would barely close, and the floor was so strewn with toys it was nearly impossible to walk!

Gifts Galore

As for all those well-intentioned baby gifts I mentioned earlier? Before you set up your nursery, please realize that just because someone gives you a cute baby gift, if it's not something you will use or if it doesn't match your nursery décor, you're better off exchanging it, giving it to another mom friend, or donating it to a shelter for abused children. They will be more than happy to receive the item and put it to use. Otherwise it becomes unused clutter that's just taking up space in your small home. Of course, it's also fine to ask for a baby shower where, in lieu of gifts, monetary donations are made to a favorite children's charity or to your child's college savings fund.

Your *KISS* Plan

As soon as you find out you're expecting, look at magazine and internet photos of nurseries, take notes, clip pages, and make a budget and a shopping list. Sit down with your three-ring binder and your spouse and decide what room or area of the house will be the nursery and what items you need to purchase. Ideally, it's practical to have the nursery located near your master bedroom if at all possible, with a bathroom nearby.

As you plan, tour some retail stores to get ideas before you purchase anything, and remember that every store would have you believe you just *can't live without* every last piece of furniture and gadget they are marketing to you. And of course, since you want a happy life and room for your baby, it is indeed tempting. That's why you'll want to plan ahead and stick to your budget and the list in your notebook.

As you decide what to buy for your nursery, also remember that babies stay babies for a very short time before they turn into toddlers and then school-age children. It's wise to *KISS* the nursery—instead of buying a bunch of stuff that might just turn into clutter, put some of that money into your child's college fund.

Space Considerations

When you sit down with your mate and your planning binder, be sure to take and record measurements of the room to make sure all the furnishings you're planning to buy will fit properly. And like the other rooms we've discussed in this book, it's a good idea to draw out a plan for furniture arrangement, even if it's just a rough sketch. You'll also want to decide whether the room needs any fix-ups such as re-painting, caulking, or new flooring, and then budget and plan accordingly.

Some space considerations *before* you purchase anything:

- Decide which furnishings you need immediately and which ones can wait. The basics are a crib, a dresser that can also act as a changing table, a rocking chair or glider with perhaps a matching ottoman, a small table near the rocker to set a baby bottle on, lighting or a lamp, a toy box, a diaper pail, and a laundry bas-ket. Bassinets are quickly outgrown, as are changing tables, so only you can decide if those are must-have purchases for you personally and if they fit into your budget.

- Look for furniture pieces that have built-in storage. Some changing tables have shelves underneath as do some cribs.

- Consider a furniture manufacturer or store that has been around a long time and has a reputation for high-quality furnishings (e.g., Ethan Allen). These manufacturers will likely still be in business down the road, so you'll be able to add pieces that will still match your original purchases as your child grows.

- Evaluate your closet and storage space. Do you need to install shelving in the closet or buy a ready-made shelving unit or storage cabinet? Can you store per-sonal care items in stackable plastic bins and keep them under the crib ? Do you need baby clothes hangers? Take an inventory of your storage needs *before* you shop.

- Rolling plastic stackable drawers work well for storing clothes and toys and are a cost-effective alternative to a more expensive dresser. If you already have a small dresser, it's possible it might fit in the closet to allow space in the room for a rocker and ottoman.

- Armoires work well to store clothes, toys, and personal items. Use lidded stackable plastic bins on the shelves to maximize the space. Label the bins.

- Do you have relatives or friends who would be willing to give or sell you their used baby furnishings? It never hurts to ask; moms usually love to share. However, be sure to check online for the latest safety regulations before using older furnishings.

- Consider keeping the wall colors in your nursery gender-neutral so the room can grow with your child. Good neutral colors are off-white or cream, pale yellow, light green, and soft gray-blue.

- Choosing a gender-neutral flooring color is also effective long-term, and it's easier to decorate around. If you choose carpet, a multicolored Berber style won't show stains or lint much and is easy to vacuum. Hardwood or bamboo floors are also neutral and easy to clean. Avoid pink and blue carpets that become dated, and also avoid solid light-colored carpets that readily show stains.

- Decide if you want to create a theme for the room before you buy any decorative items or toys. It's more cost-effective to keep theme items to inexpensive accessories that can be replaced as your child matures. Opting for a wallpaper border, stenciling the wall, or using removable decals are all budget-friendly ways to implement a theme. It's also fun to paint stripes on the wall, and a themed rug is inexpensive and fun as well.

- Arrange the crib so that it's near the doorway. That way you don't have to tiptoe across the room when you've finally put your baby to sleep. Likewise, position the crib so that it's not in direct sunlight or near a draft.

- Arrange furniture around the perimeter of the room to keep the center of the space free for walking the baby and for future crawling and playing.

- One mother put her grandfather's rocking chair in the nursery and loved the extended family feeling of doing so. Perhaps someone in your family is ready to pass down an heirloom piece of furniture for your nursery.

- A young mother told me she purchased a crib that converted into a toddler bed as a cost-effective crib/bed option.

As you read this chapter and look at the resources list at the end, I'm confident you'll come up with solutions to your nursery furnishing and storage needs as you work through the planning process. Remember to think outside the box and get creative, always keeping your baby's safety as your first priority whether you purchase new or used items.

Gotta Get Organized

Any item or furnishing you buy will have to be stored somewhere, either now or as your child grows, so keep that in mind as you purchase goods. That's another reason why I advocate the *KISS* principle, and here are my best suggestions for organizing all the stuff for your baby's nursery.

- Don't overbuy baby clothes in too many sizes, because all babies grow at differing rates. Your little one may never wear some of the larger outfits, or they may not be the right size for the right season.

- Label lidded plastic bins for clothes you need to store for future use. If you're on a tight budget, large Pampers boxes work great as storage boxes. Write what's inside on a piece of colorful construction paper glued to the front of the box. Baskets with fabric liners also work well for storing clothes and toys, and the wicker won't snag delicate items if the baskets are fabric lined.

- Store items such as extra boxes of diapers under the crib. Skirt the crib if you don't want the containers visible.

- If you already have a changing table, use stackable plastic bins on rollers to store personal care items and diapers instead of purchasing a dresser.

- Instead of purchasing a changing table, why not buy a desk that matches the other furniture and use it as a changing table? Cover it with a changing pad, of course, and later your child can use the desk for studying.

- Over-the-door clear shoe holders work great to store personal care items because you can easily see them at a glance. They also work great for small toys.
- Plastic or wicker laundry baskets or hampers make great storage for toys and stuffed animals.
- Five-gallon white plastic buckets with handles are available from your local home renovation store and work well for storing toys and stuffed animals.
- A bookcase can hold books, and also games and toys as your child grows.
- Empty wet wipes containers work great for storing baby socks and small stuffed animals and toys. Label the front.
- Remove any of your own items from the nursery closet so you have room to store the stroller and travel crib/playpen.
- Go through baby clothes and toys every six months and weed them out to avoid clutter since *KISS* is an ongoing process. Label a large diaper box or a plastic bin *Donate* and store items there until you're ready to pass them along.
- Buy a label maker at an office supply store. It will serve you well over the years to label bins and boxes as your little one grows and the toys and clothing needs change.
- Before purchasing containers, look around your home and see if you already have things on hand that you aren't using that might work.

Beautiful Baby Bath

Hopefully your nursery will be located near a bathroom for ease. Rubber duckies and other bath gear can quickly proliferate and take over your bathroom, so nip bathroom clutter in the bud by *KISS*-ing there too!

- Buy a plastic basket or a lidded plastic bin to keep all your baby's personal bath care items in. You can either store it in the nursery and carry it to the bathroom, or store it in the bathroom closet.
- Keep a notepad in the bin or in a drawer for writing down items you need to purchase as they run out. You can also keep a magnetized notepad on your refrigerator as a master grocery shopping list.
- Keep a small plastic laundry basket in the bathtub to drain wet toys, or hang a mesh bag over the shower faucet. You can buy mesh bags in the produce section of many grocery stores.

Photo Albums and Memorabilia

From the moment a baby is born, photographs and memorabilia begin to collect. If you're digitally inclined, set up a file on your computer for digital photos and for scanning in memorabilia. If you prefer to keep hard copies of photos, file them in stackable photo boxes that come with mini-file tab dividers and store them until you're ready to put them into albums. Label the file tabs by date and event, and label the front of the box as well. You can do the same with larger memorabilia by putting labeled hanging file folders in a file bin.

Even if you don't have the time or propensity for making scrapbooks, by having all the photos and memorabilia organized in files from the very beginning of your child's life, once your sweet bundle of joy grows up and leaves home, they'll easily be able to take their photos with them and perhaps they will be interested in making their own scrapbooks. Just last year I created scrapbooks from my own childhood using Creative Memories products, and I loved every minute of the process.

The Sound of Music

It's nice to introduce your little one to music right from the start, so why not use your preferred high-tech method of piping in some soothing tunes for your little one?

Green Baby

I know you want to give your new little bundle of joy the very best start in life. As someone who has been personally challenged with environmental sensitivities and allergies for many years, I feel compelled to tell you about the health wisdom of making your baby's nursery "green." By that I mean buying and using the least toxic furnishings and products as possible. Below are a few basic "green baby" tips to get you started, and I've also given you some product resources at the end of this chapter.

- Organic wool or cotton crib mattresses do not have flame retardant chemicals that can cause a host of health challenges, so it's best to buy an organic crib mattress.

- Use organic sheets and blankets to avoid the "no ironing needed" chemicals that are often found on commercial store-bought sheets.

- If you can't afford organic linens, which do tend to be pricey, soak new bedding in your washer, using half a gallon of vinegar and two cups of baking soda in very hot water. Then wash with a nontoxic detergent and rinse a couple of times. This helps to remove any chemicals; I do it all the time when I buy new linens and it works quite well. Sometimes it takes repeat treatments and/or soaking them overnight in the vinegar and baking soda solution.

- Avoid laundering your baby's bedding or clothing with scented detergents or fabric softeners because some fragrances can trigger asthma and allergies.

- Use chlorine-free and fragrance-free baby diapers and wet wipes.

- Only clean your baby's room with nontoxic household cleaners that are fragrance-free. Avoid commercial cleaning products.

- Never use scented carpet cleaners; steam clean with hot water only. Your carpet cleaner can be trained to do it this way.

- Avoid plug-in air fresheners and air freshener sprays that can trigger asthma and allergies.

- Use nontoxic and fragrance-free personal care products made especially for infants.
- Buy an air purifier.
- Provide nontoxic natural cloth and wooden toys instead of plastic ones.
- Stay away from new carpeting that outgases chemicals. Better to steam clean the current carpeting in the room (use water only—no fragranced detergents) or to install hardwood flooring, cork, or natural linoleum.
- Aluminum mini-blinds are a nice clean window treatment available in many colors.
- Paint the room with no-VOC paint at least two months before the birth. And Mom, please don't paint the room yourself while you're pregnant.

As we end this chapter, I wish you great fun and happiness as you set up your nursery during this wonderful time in your life. If you keep the *KISS* principle in mind, you and your little dear one will be on your way to a serene and soothing space.

Resources for a Small Baby Nursery

Air Purifiers
www.IQAir.com

Baby Furniture
www.EthanAllen.com
www.SimplyBabyFurniture.com
www.USABaby.com

Closet Shelving
www.ContainerStore.com
www.Elfa.com
www.Ikea.com

Crib Skirts
www.BabyBedding.com
www.PotteryBarnKids.com

Fabric-Lined Wicker Baskets
www.HomeGoods.com
www.Michaels.com
www.TJMaxx.com

Gently Used Baby Goods
www.Gently-Used.com

Green Flooring and Home Improvement Supplies
www.BioShieldPaint.com
www.CaliforniaBaby.com (showroom in Los Angeles)
www.GreenBuildingSupply.com

Nontoxic Baby Personal Care
www.CaliforniaBaby.com
www.SaffronRouge.com

Nontoxic Household Cleaners
www.SeventhGeneration.com

Nontoxic Paint
www.BenjaminMoore.com
www.BioShieldPaint.com
www.Sherwin-Williams.com

Organic Baby Furniture, Linens, Products, and Toys
www.GreenNest.com
www.Lifekind.com
www.PureRest.com

Over-the-Door Shoe Pockets
www.ContainerStore.com
www.OrganizedAtoZ.com
www.Target.com

Photo Albums/Boxes and Scrapbook Supplies
www.CreativeMemories.com
www.ExposuresOnline.com
www.Michaels.com

Rolling Plastic Stackable Drawers
www.ContainerStore.com
www.ShopGetOrganized.com
www.Target.com

Wall Decals
www.PotteryBarnKids.com
www.RoommatesPeelandStick.com
www.WallStickerOutlet.com

--- YOUR SMALL SPACE NOTES ---

13

Honey, I Shrunk the Kids' Room

Your wee little baby we prepared for in the last chapter has quickly grown into a child. One of the greatest gifts you can give your children in life is to teach them from a young age how to organize their own bedroom, because an orderly room is their pleasant haven from which they experience the fullness of their unique life. As your kids grow, the organizing skills you teach them as a parent will serve them well. (Who knows, your organized child of today may become your successful CEO, doctor, or astronaut son or daughter of tomorrow!)

All Kids Can Learn

Please never think for a moment that young children can't learn organizing skills, because *they can*. As a former certified school teacher and tutor who has taught every age from kindergarten to teens to adults, I can vouch that even kindergarteners can learn some organizing skills. In fact, it's been my experience that most children like to learn how to organize things if someone is willing to teach them, and they are proud of themselves when they are praised for doing so.

Keys to Success

One of the keys to success in organizing your child's room, no matter what their age, is to enlist their help as is age-appropriate. Gently teach or coach them along rather than doing it for them just because "it's easier for you to do it yourself." Remember, *they need to learn*. Be sure to make it fun and perhaps offer a reward like lunch out together or an ice cream cone after you're done. Praise their efforts often and don't criticize them. Keep in mind that every child is different, so observe your child and plan accordingly to their personality and age. And once again, as you set up your child's room for maximum rest and enjoyment, their safety should always be your first priority.

Real-Life Kids

What exactly should you take into account about your child's particular personality when helping them organize their room? Well, for one, have realistic expectations, because although every child *can* get organized, not all have a natural penchant for it, so it will take a little more work and patience on your part. And some children also have learning or attention issues, so you may need to settle for a room that's "organized enough." Kids are not adults; they're active children who are a work in progress, so don't expect perfection. As children mature, they can be expected to be more organized than when they are young children.

Vive la Différence

To illustrate the differences between kids and their penchant (or lack thereof) for organization, here's a real-life example that you'll be able to relate to if you think about your own children, or those you know.

I once knew a mother whose very logical eleven-year-old daughter was so naturally organized that every hanger in her closet faced the same way and there was not a piece of paper in sight on her study desk. (*Yes, really!*) Contrast that to her highly creative nine-year-old son who continually stored ice cream bar wrappers under his bed and left soiled clothes lying on the floor of his closet, much to his (fastidiously organized) mother's chagrin. The point being, every child has a different organizational style, or lack of it, so go with the flow and work around the personality of your particular child.

Small Bedroom Challenges

A small bedroom for a child in the twenty-first century can pose organizational challenges. What with everything from mountains of toys to their own TVs, computers, and electronic games—not to mention prolific rock and seashell collections and school papers—kids' rooms can quickly become overloaded clutter castles. But it doesn't have to be that way. Once again, the big "organizing secret" is to realize you only have so much room, and *make wise choices*. In other words, practice the *KISS* principle: "Keep It Super Simple!"

The main organizational goal for your child's room is to set up systems and arrange furnishings so that everything has its own place. Of course, it's only in a perfect world that kids will *keep* everything in its place, because they are, after all, *kids*. The important thing is that there is a *base* of organization, which means there are systems and containers in place to store their belongings. With just a "quick pickup" after a busy day of playing and studying, order can be achieved rather easily.

As you make this transition and turn the nursery into a child's room, begin by evaluating the space. What pieces of furniture do you have that can be used, and which ones may need to be stored, donated, or sold? What baby theme items need to be donated, and what should replace them that's more age-appropriate? Sit down again with your three-ring binder to take some notes, make a plan, and budget. Decide if the room needs any repairs, painting, or flooring updates and plan accordingly. Be sure to use nontoxic no-VOC paint. It's also a good health practice to have an air purifier in your child's room.

Fab Furnishings

As you decide which furniture to purchase, keep the long-term picture in mind and avoid cutesy and trendy furniture designed only for very young children. Sure, all those glossy magazine photos of celebrity kids' over-the-top theme rooms are dazzling and fun to look at. But I know that you are wiser with your money than the marketers hope and will instead shop carefully to purchase the best quality furnishings at the best prices.

Choose classic furniture of good quality that will serve your child from toddler through teenager. Make sure the design is timeless enough that they can take it to college and then to their first apartment. Take your child shopping with you to help pick out their own furniture, and explain why you're avoiding trendy purchases.

One special note: I'm personally a big fan of Ethan Allen furnishings and stores because of their quality furniture and timeless/classic design appeal. I consider their pieces a long-term *investment* rather than an expense. Their retail showrooms are set up like real rooms at home, so you can get a true picture of how your own room will look. Their in-store designers can help you choose furnishings that will grow with your child.

Keep furnishings for kids' rooms to the basics, choosing from the list below.

- Twin bed, with possible pull-out trundle for sleepovers (Note: It's healthiest to buy organic mattresses that are free of chemicals.)
- Twin bed, with built-in drawers underneath for clothing storage
- Bunk beds if your children share a room
- Study/computer desk, chair, and lamp, or two of each if your children share a room
- Cozy chair for reading
- Bean bag chairs for having friends over
- Dresser or armoire for clothing
- Bookcase for books, games, TV

- Rocker or reading chair
- Bulletin board for hanging art and messages
- Whiteboard or chalkboard
- Small table for young children to color and play
- Clothes hamper (tall covered wastebaskets are slim and work great inside closets)
- Adjustable closet shelving
- Nightstand and lamp by bed
- Toy boxes, trunks, or bins

Furniture Arrangement

Arrange furniture around the perimeter of the room so that maximum floor space is available for playing and for having sleepovers. Avoid placing the bed near the window where too much light might keep your child from sleeping or where they might catch a draft.

Dream Theme

As I mentioned in the previous chapter, if you want a theme room, it's best to keep the furnishings, wall color, and carpet neutral. Create the theme by using colorful accessories that are less expensive and that you can change from time to time as your child matures. Let your child choose their own theme, or at least let them help to choose it. Painting wall stripes, using removable wall decals, and a buying a themed rug are fun and inexpensive ways to change a room quickly and economically.

Zone Organizing

I like the concept of what I call "zone organizing" for teaching kids how to organize their room and keep it organized. Zone organizing avoids kids getting overwhelmed since instead of having to reorganize their whole room, they can organize one zone at a time, see results, and quickly feel successful. Start with one area (zone) below and teach your child how to organize that area. Then take a break. And when your child's room needs maintenance, ask them to tackle one zone a week to keep things streamlined and maintained over time. Zones include:

Bed. Teach your child how to make their bed the minute they get out of it, and praise them for doing so. It's easiest to provide them with a comforter and one pillow that they helped choose so that all they have to do is pull the comforter over their bed and it looks fine. Avoid "fussy" bedspreads that have to be just so or will get very wrinkled. The bed is the largest horizontal surface in a room other than the floor, so if the bed is made, the whole room looks more orderly; if it's rumpled, it's the first visual mess you notice upon entering the room.

Dresser. The dresser is a zone and individual drawers are smaller zones within that zone. Pants should be folded in one drawer, tops in another, socks and undies in another, and so forth, with no mixing of clothing types and no stuffing of unfolded items together in one drawer. Teach your child to sort their drawers by clothing type and to always fold everything. Again, show them how it's done and teach them to make it a habit, just like brushing their teeth. Use shoeboxes or plastic bins inside the drawers to keep socks and undies and small clothing items separated.

Desk. A desk encourages good study habits. Provide colorful containers for pens, pencils, stapler, and other office supplies. You can cover juice cans with colorful contact paper if your budget is tight, or buy small clay planters at your local nursery. Keep drawers neat using small plastic containers to divide supplies. Checkbook boxes also work well for this. Make sure there is a comfortable desk chair and hang a decorative hook on the wall near the desk for your child's school backpack. Finally, a plastic file bin with hanging files works great for organizing school paperwork.

Backpacks. Even though it's not a piece of furniture, I want to address backpacks in this section. As a former teacher, I can assure you that backpacks can quickly become huge clutter magnets and the bane of a parent's (and teacher's!) existence with lost homework molding away deep within their recesses (pun intended!). Train your child to declutter their backpack every day after school, making sure they have assignments out that need to be done the next day, and that they reload all the proper books into the backpack for the next day. File away any papers they want to keep as memorabilia in their treasure file box. (Refer to the story below for details on how to set up an effective school memorabilia/treasure box.)

Closet Shelves. Teach your child how to hang up their clothes immediately after taking them off, rather than dropping them on the floor, putting them on the bed, or draping them over a chair. Provide child-size hangers and hang clothes by clothing type and color (e.g., all pants together, all tops together, just like in their dresser drawers) so it's easy to get dressed. Shoes can go on shelves, on the floor in plastic bins, or in over-the-door shoe pockets. Keep a box labeled *Donations* in the closet for outgrown clothes.

Laundry Basket

A tall plastic garbage can with or without a lid works great for laundry as it's slim and fits in small closets better than round baskets. Have your child put their laundry in the basket, not on the floor, and ask them to bring their own laundry to the laundry room when the container is full. Put their laundered, folded clothes back in the garbage can and let them put their own clothes away, with or without help as is age-appropriate.

Bookcases

Most children love books and love being read to. Make sure you have a bookcase and use it to store their favorite books, as well as puzzles and games.

Toy Box

A toy box with a hinged lid is one way to store toys, but hinges can be dangerous to small fingers. You may want to opt instead for plastic stacking storage drawers, colorful plastic stacking cubes, or plastic lidded bins. Label the drawer or bin fronts with your label maker—*Stuffed Animals*, *Barbies*, *Legos*—so items are sorted by category. If your child is too young to read labels, teach them that Legos go in the green bin, stuffed animals go in the red bin, and so forth. Another option is to put a picture of the contents on the front of a plastic bin or box and cover the picture with clear contact paper so it stays put.

Sharing with Siblings

A word of wisdom regarding siblings sharing a small room: children have differing organizational capacities, styles, and needs. When Michael Messy has to share a room with Nathan Neatfreak, trouble may ensue. However, if you live in a small space home, separate bedrooms may not be an option for your kids. So you'll need to be creative about how to promote organizational harmony between siblings. Keep in mind that it will likely never be a *perfect* arrangement, but it can be a *harmoniously workable* one. Use my ideas below to help keep the peace.

Sibling Bed Bliss

When siblings share a room, I think it's wise that they each have their own bed as a private zone that is distinctly theirs. Choose two complementary colors that both kids like for their room, and let each child choose their own comforter and decorate their own bed area according to their unique tastes and theme. Don't worry that both sides don't perfectly match; it's more important that your kids are happy and are developing a sense of individuality than that their room look like a matching showplace in a decorating magazine.

Twin beds take up more floor space but can be used as a way to divide the room in half. Each child can take one side of the room for their bed, desk, and dresser as a way to carve out their unique organizing and decorating style.

Bunk beds take up less floor space, but not every child feels comfortable sleeping on the top bunk. Also, with the beds on one side of the room, all other furniture for both kids must be combined elsewhere in the room rather than giving them each a separate side. Decide on the best bed style and arrangement depending on your children's ages and personalities.

Darling Desks and Organized Papers

If more than one child is sharing a room, consider buying two identical desks and put them face-to-face with the short sides along a wall. A double-sided bookcase can stand in between the desks for privacy and storage.

Papers proliferate quickly for children. I love what my teacher friend did to organize her son's papers from the time he was in kindergarten:

> We bought a plastic bin for school papers and during the year, we tossed them all in there. Once summer came, we made it a fun ritual between mom and son to go through each paper and decide which ones were special that he wanted to keep. He was allowed only those that would fit inside one 9" x 12" gold clasp envelope that was labeled for that year's grade. We also put report cards, awards, and any newspaper clippings for sports in there. When he brought home large items like science projects, we took a photo of him with the project, put the photo in the gold envelope, and tossed the actual project. I set up a plastic lidded file bin with hanging file folders labeled Kindergarten through 12th grade and we filed the gold envelopes in there by grade for each year. I labeled the outside of the bin "John's Treasure Box." When my son left home, all his childhood memories were organized in one small bin, ready for him to take with him.

I was so touched by this mom's story about the loving bond and memories it created with her son. What a wonderful legacy that you can also easily do with your child!

Media Galore

With today's kids being so plugged in, you'll want to update your kids' rooms with enough power outlets. I feel it's ultimately up to each parent to decide how much "tech and TV" is "enough" for their particular children and family, and set up their rooms accordingly.

House Rules

Every family has "house rules" they maintain in order for home life to function at its best capacity. And for that reason it's wise to teach children that keeping their room reasonably orderly and clean, even though it's their room, is *respectful to the family*. As I've already mentioned, siblings do often have differing organizing penchants; but with mom and dad as the family leaders, an acceptable level of organization at home must be agreed upon simply out of courtesy for other family members.

Organized Enough

So what's "organized enough" for children's rooms? Ice cream wrappers should not be allowed to grow mold under the bed, nor should clothes be allowed to pile up on the floor unwashed. By the same token, a neat freak child should not be allowed to insist that their less organized sibling have all their clothing tags facing the same direction in their dresser drawer or their shoes militarily lined up in the closet. Discuss with your children a household standard of what is "organized enough" for their shared room. That way there will be harmony and both siblings can grow into the unique individuals God meant them to be.

Teen Time

All that being said about house rules, a brief word here about teen bedrooms. They should be organized using the same principles we've already talked about, but keep this in mind: most teens (I've taught them!) are at that life stage, God love 'em, where they are easing their way into independence from Mom and Dad and want to do things their way.

As a parent, decide what you can *realistically* live with that will keep your teen's best interests in mind while maintaining respectful order for the rest of the family, and go from there. For example, maybe it's simply agreeing that the door to their room must be kept closed when they are not home; but for the sake of monitoring girl/boy visits and media or computer use when teens are at home, the door absolutely remains open for parental supervision. Alas, their clutter will just have to be visible and tolerated for a bit by others in the household. Another option for both teens and younger kids might be to keep media and computers in the family room rather than in their bedrooms.

One good friend of mine told me that her boys preferred as teenagers to have Mom put their folded clothes on their bed. They then put them on the floor and wore them from there. Mom finally decided that it simply wasn't worth arguing about.

And I still remember the teen sisters' bedrooms I once helped to organize: to say their floors were deep with stuff and that their mother was tired of nagging about it would be putting it mildly. I was called in to play referee, and as we sorted, tossed, and bagged I coached the girls on how they could keep their room "organized enough" so they still felt like it was their domain, and so that their mom was not constantly screaming at them to "Clean up your room!" Mission accomplished.

Evolving Process

Staying organized is an ever-evolving process, so once every six months or so you'll want to go through your child's room with them and assess what toys, clothes, books, and games need to be donated, stored, or given away. Remember that by using the *KISS* principle, you'll have less stuff to go through to begin with! Always donate kids' toys and outgrown clothing to charity, family, or friends rather than tossing items you no longer want or need in the trash. Your children learn by example, and this will teach them early on to "go green."

Kids' Room Closing

I'm so glad we've been able to spend time together here for your kids' rooms. I hope you'll take the organizing tips and ideas I've offered and use them to teach your children good organizing skills that will serve them for the rest of their lives.

Resources for Children's Small Rooms

Air Purifiers
www.IQAir.com

Children's Furniture
www.EthanAllen.com
www.PotteryBarnKids.com

Closet Shelving
www.ContainerStore.com
www.Elfa.com
www.Ikea.com

Green/Organic Children's Furniture, Linens, Mattresses, Toys
www.GreenNest.com
www.LifeKind.com
www.PureRest.com

Interior Design for Baby through Teen Rooms
www.BeachBungalowDesigns.com

Nontoxic/No-VOC Paint
www.BenjaminMoore.com
www.BioShieldPaint.com
www.Sherwin-Williams.com

Organic Mattresses
www.GreenNest.com
www.LifeKind.com
www.PureRest.com

Storage Bins/Crates
www.ContainerStore.com
www.OrganizedAtoZ.com
www.Target.com

YOUR SMALL SPACE NOTES

Hobbies, Crafts, Mementos, and Sports Gear, *Oh My!*

If you think that just because you live in a small space home you can't have indoor hobbies or save any treasured mementos, I'd like to reassure you that it's just *not true*. What *is* true is that since your home is small, you'll need to once again practice the *KISS* principle: "Keep It Super Simple!"

Suzy Selective

There's one thing I'm adamant about regarding crafts and memorabilia, and I speak both from personal experience and from observing my creative friends. There's just no getting around the fact that you'll *definitely* need to be selective about how many hobbies you can realistically take on in your small space and about how much memorabilia you can keep and store efficiently.

Please don't make the mistake I did as a college girl of eighteen who went off to New York to be a nanny. I carted four large cardboard boxes of personal keepsakes with me because I wasn't sure whether I was going to stay for a summer or longer, and apparently I was afraid of feeling homesick. Included in the stash were my high school dance corsages (long wilted), my cheerleading jacket (long ago too small), and a bracelet engraved *I'll Never Forget You* from my first junior high school boyfriend (long gone!).

All these years and relocations later, I can honestly tell you (and recommend to you as well) that I've happily narrowed my personal memorabilia down to one small decorative plastic "treasure box," plus just one 12″ × 12″ scrapbook for every ten years of my life. And God bless my dear hubby, who last year finally donated his old high school football trophies to the dumpster after I found them a bit moldy while cleaning out the one small storage closet in our home office!

So come on, let's get started organizing *your* crafts, memorabilia, and sports equipment.

Crazy for Crafts

As a young bride, I became "crazy for crafts." I was so excited by all the pretty supplies and fun tools that I didn't plan ahead spacewise for all the stuff that would go with the afghan knitting, the ceramics painting, the curtain sewing, and the decoupage. Lessons learned: choose no more than two crafts at a time as your passion, and don't begin another craft unless you're willing to let go of an existing craft and the supplies that go with it. Your small space, your mate, your wallet, and your sanity will all thank you!

Craftily Organized

It's wise to organize your craft supplies and tools rather than leave them helter-skelter, because organizing them actually frees you to be *more* creative. Don't make the mistake (or excuse) of thinking that if you're creative, you can't be organized. The secret is to set up systems that work for *you*, because there's not one perfect way to organize crafts.

Knitting, Sewing, or Scrapbooking

Whether it's sewing, scrapbooking, stamp collecting, knitting, or whatever, here are my favorite strategies, tips, and ideas for organizing your crafts and hobbies so that you can better enjoy them. Once again, get out your three-ring binder, take notes, and make a plan and budget.

- Set up your craft area where you will have quiet to work and where you won't be imposing your supplies on your family. If you live in a studio apartment, obviously you'll have less room than if you live in a small two-bedroom house with a garage, so choose your particular hobby accordingly.
- One of the best ways to get an idea of how to organize your craft area in your home is to visit your local craft, art, and scrapbook stores and study how they have things organized. Take a notepad, walk around, observe, write down ideas. You'll want your little craft area at home to look similar

to a craft boutique once you're done setting it up. You can also take your camera along to the store, but be sure to ask the owner for permission to take photos.

- Again, remember the *KISS* principle at all times during your planning and shopping process. If you're going to become a scrapbooker, for example, don't buy twelve albums and ten large packets of pretty papers right at the outset. Focus on one small project at a time, buy the supplies for that project, finish it, and move on to the next project.

- Decide what furnishings and tools you will need and establish a budget *after* looking around your home to see if you already have items you might be able to use. For example, a card table can be set up as a work station, and you can store supplies in plastic lidded bins or labeled shoe boxes underneath it.

- Once you've evaluated what you already have, make a list of what you think you still need *before* you go shopping. Buy the furnishings you need first, the supplies and tools for your crafts next, and then choose storage containers so you don't buy more containers than you really need or have room for.

- If you have a *very* tiny area in your home to set up for crafts/hobbies, consider converting an office or computer armoire into a small craft center. Armoires have shelving, dividers, and drawers, and you can shut the doors so that your mess is out of sight when you're not working on your project. You can also buy ready-made craft armoires. See the resource section at the end of this chapter for more information.

- Label every storage container, bin, and drawer with a handheld label maker that you can purchase at an office supply store. It will keep everything looking neat because the labels will be uniform and easier to read than handwritten ones.

- Clear stackable plastic drawers work great for sorting items like sewing fabric and scrapbook paper.

- Accordion file holders work great for sorting and storing sewing patterns.

- Photo boxes are superb for storing photos that you're going to put into scrapbooks, but they work for storing craft supplies too. They stack well on shelves because they're a uniform size. Photo boxes also come in a variety of colors and patterns and are inexpensive.

- Canning jars or plastic food containers work well for holding craft items such as embroidery threads, beads, and whatnot. Fishing tackle boxes also make wonderful sorters for small craft items. Get creative!

- A pegboard hanging on the wall over your worktable makes a dandy visual way to organize your craft tools. You can even draw around each tool with a black magic marker so you'll know right where to put the tool back.

- If you only have a tiny corner to use, hide your work area behind a decorative folding screen. Or use two bookcases as a room partition and place your storage bins on the shelves.

- A friend of mine bought an old library card catalog for all her sewing notions, labeled the drawer fronts, and used it for a coffee table in front of the loveseat where she sat to knit. Dandy!

- Use the walls around your work area for storing containers and bins. Placing two tall bookcases on either side of your worktable or desk keeps everything right at your fingertips.

- An ironing board that hangs over the door saves space, as do under-the-bed plastic storage bins and over-the-door clear plastic shoe holders.

- Be sure you have adequate overhead and task lighting, as well as enough electrical outlets. And don't forget a trash can.

- If you already have a craft area that's messy in your home, start organizing it by weeding through your tools and supplies and donating or tossing any you no longer need. That's a priority. Then organize what's left, using my ideas above. Focusing on one small area at a time, work for two hours and then take a break.

Keepsake Love

Oh what to do, what to do, with all of your memorabilia? Never fear, there's hope for organizing it within your small home space. And if you're a young person just starting out, you're a step ahead of everyone else by getting it sorted and systematized early on—*before* it gets out of control.

Kids' Artwork and School Papers

In chapter 13, I mentioned a fabulously simple and compact system that a teacher friend of mine set up for her son to sort and store all of his school artwork and memorabilia. Refer back to page 202 to refresh that idea in your mind.

Gracious Gifts

Indeed, you not only have your own crafts and such to deal with, but what about gifts you receive from others, such as Aunt Jane's well-intentioned handmade doodad that doesn't fit in with your décor *at all*? Some effective ways of preventing gift clutter are to accept any gift with a gracious smile, but if it's just not your style then immediately donate it to charity without a peep from you to the gift giver or anyone who knows them. You might also make an arrangement with loved ones to exchange cards rather than gifts, or to make donations to each others' favorite charities.

Photos

Digital Photos

Photos can proliferate at the speed of light with today's digital cameras and phones that have cameras built in. Set up file folders on your computer that are labeled and sorted in a way that makes sense to you. When you upload photos onto your computer, immediately delete bad shots and organize the good ones into the file folders.

If in the future you're planning to put your photos into online or paper scrapbooks, crop the photos at that time. Once a year go through all the photos on your computer and be sure you still want all of them. Delete any you no longer want to keep. Also, be sure to back up your computer regularly.

Paper Photos

If you prefer paper photos, the easiest way to organize them quickly is to put them in rectangular photo boxes. Again, toss any bad shots, label the photos on the back, label the envelopes they were developed in, and file them in order by month and year using the dividers that come with the photo box. If you want to label each photo on the back, Creative Memories makes a pencil to write on the back of photos without damaging them. When you store your photos in labeled photo boxes, when (and if) you want to create scrapbooks, you'll be ready.

The best way to stay on top of organizing your photos? Simple. Take fewer photos to begin with. Not maybe what you (or I!) wanted to hear, but true.

Memorabilia Madness

With memorabilia, the key is the big "D" word: *decide.* You simply cannot keep every wedding invitation, greeting card, and sports letter jacket emblem that accrues over a lifetime of many years, especially when you live in a small space home. Just like you, I'm a very sentimental person with a big heart, but after so many relocations I've learned the hard way that it's far more rewarding to choose the most heartfelt items and ditch the rest before it becomes "memorabilia madness" for your heirs to take to the dump.

My Best Memorabilia Organizing Ideas

When I turned the big 5-0, I realized my life was likely at least half over and I felt an increasing need to turn all those keepsake items I'd saved into something pretty that I could sit down and look at when the spirit moved me. I decided that I was finally going to give myself the gift of creating a photo autobiography by making scrapbooks about my life that I could enjoy in my golden years.

My Scrapbook M.O.

I bought one 12″ × 12″ Creative Memories photo album for every decade of my life, and I only put in there what was truly meaningful to me. I tossed the rest. I especially like the Creative Memories scrapbook company for their quality and selection. They have wonderful products, classes, and dedicated leaders who, for a small fee, can teach you how to do what I did. I've been a fan of theirs for years.

In my scrapbooks, I used pocket-style pages for items that were bulky, like the emblem from my high school cheerleading outfit. I put items that weren't paper, like flat award medals, right onto the page, and I also put newspaper clippings on the page with special adhesives from Creative Memories. I took photos of large items that were too big to keep but that I wanted to remember, put the photo in the scrapbook, and tossed the large memorabilia. I absolutely love my finished scrapbooks and they save storage space.

Hatbox Storage and Binder Bliss

Remember how I said memorabilia organizing is largely about deciding what to keep and what to toss? Well, here's another little secret: some of it simply won't fit in scrapbooks, *and* you can't take a picture of it, *but* you still want to keep it.

Here's an example of what I mean. Some of my greatest treasures are the love letters my husband and I wrote to each other during our courtship, which began when we were just eighteen and nineteen years old. You'd have thought no two people had ever fallen so in love (other than maybe Romeo and Juliet!), and we wrote letters and notes to each other often.

Since our big stack of love letters didn't fit in my scrapbooks and I wasn't willing to part with even one of them, I bought a beautiful round floral hatbox to store them in. I put them in order by postmark date and tied them together with colorful ribbons. My hubby and I still give each other greeting cards often, and I store them the same way. Another way to store letters and cards is to put them into a three-ring notebook. Organize them by date and insert them into clear sheet protectors, then store the labeled binder on a bookshelf.

The point here is that if you have things that are *truly* heartfelt to you, you *should* keep them. You just have to be selective and find ways to keep them in a *compact way.* For instance, your wedding dress can be made into decorative pillows or pieces of it can be framed with conservation framing materials. A salvageable piece of your grandmother's tattered quilt can be mounted in a shadow box. And wonderful acrylic display boxes are available to mount the football that earned you that touchdown in high school.

Latest Sports Announcement

As we wind down this chapter, I have two real-life emails from friends to share with you about sports and all the equipment and memorabilia that goes with that "magnificent obsession."

Gloria—Golf Wife and Memorabilia Mom

My friend Gloria is married to a golf pro kind of guy, and she's also the devoted mother of two kids who love sports and competitions. She writes:

> Dear Kathryn,
>   Don't even go there about sports equipment and memorabilia! Our basement has enough golf bags to supply every person in this world with clubs! Oh, and just ask my fifty-nine-year-old brother the story about his collection of Mickey Mantel baseball cards that got lost or tossed when we moved once and he says he could be rich today if not! As for our daughter's memorabilia, she has a hernia-sized pile of scrapbooks! Help! —Gloria

Baseball Bob (a.k.a. Organized Ethan)

A guy friend of mine is living proof that you don't have to be sports deprived just because you live in a small urban apartment. Not only that, you can be uber-organized with all the memorabilia, equipment, and gear that goes along with your passion! I was so impressed by a young boy being this organized that I asked if I could share his story with you in the hopes that it will give you real-life ideas for your own favorite sport, whatever that may be. He said:

Hi Kathryn,

The trophies I earned were mostly from Little League baseball, and they were kept on a shelf in my room and uniforms were kept in my closet. Like many boys, I collected baseball cards. I scotch-taped some of them onto blank pages of an already bound art-type book (which was probably meant for drawings). I attended some pro baseball games with my dad and numerous basketball games with a friend. I kept programs from many of these games in the chest of drawers in my room in our apartment. In fact, I believe I still have a program or two, complete with autographs, in storage today from the late 70s. As far as sports gear, which was a baseball glove, ball, bat, and basketball, I stored these in a toy chest in my room. Hope this helps your readers! —Ethan

For more tips and ideas about storing sports gear, see chapter 17 about garage storage.

Resources for Small Hobby Spaces

Armoires Designed for Hobbies
www.Amazon.com
www.OverStock.com
www.Sauder.com

Craft Tables
www.SewingTableShop.com
www.StacksandStacks.com
www.WalMart.com

Decorative Folding Screens
www.BallardDesigns.com
www.HomeDecorators.com

Hatboxes
www.HomeGoods.com
www.Marshalls.com
www.TJMaxx.com

Over-the-Door Ironing Boards
www.BedBathandBeyond.com
www.ShopGetOrganized.com
www.WalMart.com

Over-the-Door Shoe Pockets
www.ContainerStore.com
www.Target.com
www.WalMart.com

Photo Storage and Scrapbook Supplies
www.CreativeMemories.com
www.ExposuresOnline.com
www.Michaels.com

Plastic Bins and Rolling Drawers
www.ContainerStore.com
www.Target.com
www.WalMart.com

YOUR SMALL SPACE NOTES

15

Laundry Rooms, Libraries, and Beverage Bars

Special Small Spaces

Laundry Room Love

TV commercials would have you believe that there's romantic rapture in spending your entire weekend snuggled up to their high-sudsing laundry detergent. But if you're anything like me, seeing your whites get whiter has never rated especially high on the list of life's pleasurable activities, especially if you're using a tiny laundry room or have a small stackable washer and dryer tucked away in a hall closet.

I've learned over the years that the key to doing laundry in a small space home is . . . you guessed it . . . use the *KISS* principle . . . *Keep It Super Simple!* I've greatly increased my personal laundry pleasure quotient by simplifying and organizing my wardrobe, laundry processes, and space. You can easily adapt my tips and strategies below to make them work for you.

Simplify Your Wardrobe

The key to getting your laundry area under control in a small space doesn't start with your laundry room or lack of one; it starts with the size and type of your wardrobe. If you simplify your wardrobe to wash-and-wear, mix-and-match solid colors and limit the number of clothes you buy and the range of colors you buy them in, you'll automatically reduce laundry overwhelm. (Refer to chapter 10 to refresh yourself on how to organize and simplify your master bedroom closet and wardrobe.) Here's what I mean.

I have only two hanging rods of clothing in my small walk-in closet—one rod on the top and one on the bottom, each about five feet long. (Ditto for my hubby on the opposite side of our shared closet; we call it our "Bechen Boutique.") My two hanging rods, some stacking plastic drawers for undies, and an over-the-door shoe holder are my entire wardrobe, and I couldn't be happier. Does that mean I have a bland, boring wardrobe? *No!* Everything mixes and matches and is well organized, so I can go from casual day wear to chic day wear to an elegant evening outfit in a short amount of time as the need arises. I primarily stick to black pants, skirts, and jackets, and sleeveless pastel solid-colored shells to add some color and a feminine lace neckline. In addition, I have three cotton-knit casual outfits, and I top all my outfits off with nice jewelry and/or a pretty scarf or shawl. Because all of my clothes are wash-and-wear instead of dry-clean, I can do my laundry with ease and I seldom have to iron anything.

My hubby's wardrobe is similar. He wears mostly khaki, navy, and black dress pants with light blue, navy, and black polo shirts for work, and he has one pair of jeans and one pair of khakis for the weekends that he can wear with the same polo shirts. Two suits for important business meetings, two white dress shirts, and four classic ties hang in zippered canvas bags. I think he always looks well-groomed, and doing his laundry is also a breeze.

The point here is that if you simplify your wardrobe in a way that fits your lifestyle, you'll keep your laundry under better control and have less frustration.

Hamper Heaven

Every family member should have their own laundry hamper in their bedroom, even young children. I prefer tall plastic kitchen garbage cans with a lid that are kept in each person's clothing closet rather than in the bathroom. Because they are slim, hampers take up less floor space in the closet than round or square laundry baskets. Always put your clothes in the hamper immediately after taking them off, unless you choose to wear them another time. In that case, hang them up immediately. Teach your children to do this from a young age and buy a stain stick for every family member to keep by their hamper. When you get a stain, use the stain stick and wash the garment immediately if possible.

Daily Laundry

Even with only two of us in our household, we do one or two loads of laundry every day in the morning and evening. Most families need to do at least two to four loads of laundry a day to stay on top of it. I like doing some every day so that I always have the clothes ready to wear, and so that I don't become overwhelmed and spend all day Saturday sorting, washing, drying, and putting clothes away. I also find that if you do laundry every day, you need fewer clothes. Some people choose to do their laundry all in one day, one day a week, and they like that method. The choice is yours.

Laundry Love

At the risk of igniting World War III, I'll boldly declare here that other than very young children, every family member should do their own laundry, including their towels. With so many families in which both parents work and kids attend many activities, it's only fair that Mom not have to do it all. And who knows their own clothing better than the person who wears it? If you're struggling with who uses the washer when, assign a day of the week to each family member. Then put one or two loads in before and one or two loads in after work or school on your assigned day.

Towel Tidbit

Two full sets of towels—bath towel, hand towel, and washcloth—per family member are enough if you do laundry every day. There are two schools of thought on towel color. Either buy every towel in the house the same color so you don't have to worry about matching them up, or assign a different color to each family member. I use white and taupe towels because white towels can be bleached and taupe towels don't show things such as makeup stains.

Sorta Sorta Sorting

During my thirty years of marriage, I'll confess that I've had some white underwear turn pink. The culprit? My hubby! (No, my love, red T-shirts don't go in with white lacy panties when you're sorting clothes!) And while it *was* sweet of my man to do my laundry, after the pink undies incident and a couple loads where my clothes shrunk to a size 2 (which I haven't been since I was age two!), I came up with the concept of each family member doing their own laundry. Sort your clothes into four colors: whites, darks, bright colors, pastels. That should do you just fine.

Going Green

Use fragrance-free, nontoxic laundry detergent and fabric softeners. Your health, and our planet, will thank you! (See the resources section at the end of this chapter.)

Avoid Laundry Lunacy

If you have a tiny laundry area, here's how to organize it:

- Make sure you have a shelf or two above or next to the washer and dryer for things like laundry soap, stain sticks, bleach, fabric softeners, and nontoxic fabric brightener. Keep a backup supply of products.

- Keep hangers nearby so when you take clothes out of the dryer, they can be immediately hung up, avoiding ironing. I have a rod above my washer and dryer, plus I have an over-the-door hanger holder on the bedroom door next to my laundry closet. I keep hangers on the rod above the washer and dryer so I can hang clothes immediately, then I put them on the holder over the door. Once the whole load is hung, I take them immediately to our bedroom closet. Laundry isn't considered "done" in our home unless the clothes are put away neatly in the closet.

- Every family member should sort their clothes in their bedroom and bring one load to the washer at a time. Wash, dry, and put away immediately.

- Use the top of your dryer for folding.

- Keep wet wipes on hand and wipe down your washer and dryer once a week.

- If you have a stackable washer and dryer, designate a shelf in a nearby closet for laundry products. Lay your clothes on your bed to fold or hang and put them away immediately.

- I like space-saver style over-the-door ironing boards because you just pull them down for a quick ironing and flip them back up when you're done. No having to get out and set up a big ironing board. I also like wall-mounted iron hangers so that I can hang my iron back up even when it's not fully cool. (See the resources section at the end of this chapter.)

If you follow a laundry routine and keep your laundry area organized and clean, you'll avoid "laundry lunacy." *Truly.*

Small Space Libraries

Is there anything cozier than a home library that's well organized in attractive bookcases, with decorative objects and art
displayed as part of the interesting mix? Hardly anything has
brought me more pleasure over the years than creating my
own personal library, and I have friends and clients who feel
the same way. Snuggled on the sofa with a soft blanket, a cup
of tea, and a good book, one can escape from the cares of the
day for at least a little while.

Even if you live in a one-bedroom or a studio apartment,
you *can* have a library in your small space home. When we
lived in our tiny 20' × 20' newlywed house, I started my personal library. It was simply a 3' × 4' pretty carved wooden
bookcase I bought at an antique auction, and on it I housed
my college texts and a few novels.

Starting Your Little Library

If you stack a few books on the coffee table in your studio
apartment or on top of your foyer table with some lovely
art objects as part of the display, you've started a personal
library—not to mention you've added immediate charm to
your home. If you want a bigger library than that, I recommend placing bookcases along one whole wall of your living
room. This is especially effective in a studio apartment because it lends a cozy feeling and is also a great way to showcase knickknacks all in one place. I have created a long library
wall in several small home spaces we've lived in. It added
ambience to my room and enabled me to have all my books
at my fingertips, plus we've had many compliments about

the organized arrangement of books mixed in with our art and travel collectibles.

Blooming Bookcases

Start planning and organizing your personal library in your small space by evaluating, weeding, and sorting your existing books. Sort fiction from nonfiction first. As you look through your books, decide which ones you want to keep and donate the ones you no longer want to your church or public library, or to a local thrift store.

Once you've figured out how many books you have, here's a general rule of thumb for purchasing bookcases: each linear foot of shelving will hold about eight to twelve average hardcover novels, or six to eight large reference books like dictionaries and decorating books. No shelf should extend more than forty inches between supports to avoid shelf sagging. Remember that your collection will likely grow, so allow some extra space for new books.

Bookcase Placement

Look around your home and decide where you want to put your bookcases. They don't all have to go in the same room, but I recommend buying the same style no matter how many you purchase. That way, in the event you ever move and want to create one whole "library wall" in a living room, they'll all be the same size and style. Be sure to buy bookcases that are not only functional but that also fit your personal style and taste. Also, take into consideration that if you are starting a long-term library, you'll want to choose classic style bookcases that will evolve with your décor as your taste changes over the years.

Bookcase Safety

A quick word about safety. A bookcase full of books is heavy and can topple over. Before you load the books onto the shelves, be sure that you securely anchor the shelves to the wall. I live in Southern California, a.k.a. earthquake country, and believe me, when we had a pretty big quake last year, I was glad my hubby had securely anchored my tall bookcase towers when we moved into our high-rise home.

Organizing Bookcase Shelves

Organizing your bookshelves is a matter of personal preference. You'll for sure want to separate fiction from nonfiction, and I recommend shelving the fiction books first by category (e.g., romance, westerns, mysteries) and then alphabetically by author's last name. For nonfiction, it's best to organize your books by category (e.g., decorating, religion, travel) and then put them in an order that will enable you to quickly find them. I personally like my nonfiction books in order by height and size because they fit on the shelves better, and I don't mind visually scanning the spines to find the title I want. Others prefer them in order by author's last name or by title.

Having worked in five libraries over the years, I don't recommend an elaborate Dewey Decimal filing system for a personal library. In light of the *KISS* principle that we've talked about all through this book, it's too complicated, even if your books do take up one whole wall in your living room. Ditto for complex computer classification systems.

Special Book Arrangements

Books don't have to be confined to just one area of your home. There are pros and cons to having them all in one room, or not. If they're all on one long shelf along the living room wall, they're usually easy to find since they're all in one place. But if you put them in the rooms where you might read them, that's workable too. A combination of both also works well. For instance, I have a long library wall in my living room, but I like to read my Christian inspirational books before I go to bed. So in our bedroom I moved two bookcase towers to either side of the TV cabinet, which is opposite the foot of our bed. I like the cozy bedroom "library look" from a decorative point of view, and my books are close by for quick reading in bed. In my bathroom I have a stack of "spa books" in a basket because I like to read while having a bubble bath soak in my tub. In my living room I have a basket of decorating books near the sofa. It all works.

A word about children's books. I think kids' books should be kept in their rooms on a short bookshelf so they can reach them. If they want to read them with you on the living room sofa, that's great, but teach them to return books to the proper shelf in their bedroom once you're done.

Look around your home and see where you can add books so that they are handy for you to read while also adding a nice touch to your décor. Books look lovely stacked on top of a tufted ottoman or tucked into a cute little shelf in an alcove. The possibilities are endless. Just remember to keep them in some kind of simple yet orderly system, be it a bookcase, a basket, or stacked on a table.

Crazy for Cookbooks

Cookbooks are best stored in the kitchen if you have room. Using decorative bookends with ten or so cookbooks in between adds a nice bistro ambience to your counter. Or remove the cabinet doors over your microwave that's above your range and create a little cookbook library there. That space is usually the perfect height and will look interesting and customized, plus your cookbooks will be handy for cooking. You can also store your cookbooks nicely by stacking a few horizontally on top of your fridge.

Weeding Your Books

I recommend you weed your book collection every six months or once a year, donate what you no longer want, and then reorganize the rest. Wise words from an obsessive book collector (me!): Before I moved to California I had collected nearly a thousand books that were housed on long library wall shelves in the living room of our small apartment. After moving them all across the country several years ago and setting up my library in a new space more than once, I learned to weed my books every six months to better keep my collection under control and the cost of moving down. I'm much happier with the (five hundred or so!) books I now have—both in quantity *and* in quality.

Going Green

Always donate the books you no longer want to a library, a friend, or a charity rather than tossing them in the trash. And one last word of wisdom about personal libraries, especially for small spaces: *e-readers*.

Beverage Bar Bliss

It's fun to have a beverage bar in your home, even if your space is limited. I collected magazine photos for quite some time of those chic little bars set up in Manhattan high-rises, complete with silver ice buckets and sparkling bottles of bubbly. They looked so glamorous! So one day I pulled out my file folder of magazine photos, studied them, and with about a hundred dollars in hand, off I went to T J Maxx. There I scored a cute small table with a wooden top, scrolled metal sides, and an open area underneath. It was perfect for my beverage bar.

I found my glass ice bucket in my kitchen and bought fun glow-green palm tree stir sticks, colorful striped straws, and stemmed clear glasses. I arranged them artfully next to some bottles of Fiji water, sparkling cider, and Perrier. I filled two pretty cut crystal bowls with mixed nuts and chocolate kisses. Underneath the table I placed a decorative planter that held more bottles of sparkling cider. Slowly my little bar took shape and added a glamour touch to my small high-rise living room. I felt like I was living in a Manhattan high-rise in California. Great fun!

Once again, look around your home; maybe you already have a small table, bookcase, or dresser that you can turn into a cute little mini-bar. You can also buy ready-made bars in every price range. See the resources section at the end of this chapter.

Special Small Spaces

We've completed another chapter in our quest to get your small space home organized! I hope I've motivated and inspired you to creatively organize and streamline the special small areas in your home so they will further support your small space lifestyle with ease and comfort.

Resources for Small Space Laundry Rooms, Libraries, and Beverage Bars

Bookcases
www.HomeDecorators.com
www.Ikea.com
www.Levenger.com

Closet Organizing Consulting (Virtual)
www.NAPO.net

Nontoxic/Organic Laundry Detergent
www.Amazon.com
www.SeventhGeneration.com

Over-the-Door Hanger Holders
www.Amazon.com
www.OvertheDoor.com
www.SpaceSavers.com

Over-the-Door Ironing Boards and Iron Holders
www.Amazon.com
www.Target.com
www.WalMart.com

Ready-Made Wet Bars
www.NextTag.com
www.PotteryBarn.com

Stackable Washers and Dryers
www.CompactAppliance.com
www.Lowes.com
www.Sears.com

Wardrobe Consulting (Virtual)
www.Aici.org

YOUR SMALL SPACE NOTES

_____

_____

_____

_____

_____

_____

_____

_____

_____

_____

_____

_____

_____

_____

_____

_____

_____

_____

16

The Great, but *Small,* Outdoors

Organizing Patios and Terraces

Why not turn your small patio or terrace into a lovely garden-like retreat where you can escape for a cup of cappuccino? Or how about creating a fun and relaxing outdoor "room" for your entire family that functions as a complementary extension of your indoor space?

Outdoor Function

Almost every small home space I've ever lived in has had a small (or tiny) patio, terrace, or balcony, so I know firsthand that organizing is key to creating a space that functions well and is enjoyable. With a little ingenuity and elbow grease, you *can* turn your little space into a petite paradise.

Before you begin any work or purchase any organizing containers, supplies, or furniture, be sure to think through how you want to use the space. In other words, what's its *function*? Do you want to sit out there all alone and enjoy the birds and a few pots of flowers while you read a book? Have a romantic bistro-like dinner for two? Play board games with your family? Lounge in a hammock or swing and look up at the stars? Entertain friends with a barbecue? These are important questions because just like an indoor room, how you want to *use* the outdoor space determines the best way to organize and arrange it, and function also impacts what you'll need to buy.

Make a Plan, Jan!

Once you've decided how you'll use your outdoor space, once again pull out your three-ring binder and take some notes while you brainstorm; make a written plan for organizing and arranging things and for purchasing supplies and furnishings. Study home magazines and Google "outdoor rooms." Print out photos that appeal to you and keep them in your binder. You can also get ideas online by looking at photos on the garden center pages of such sites as www.Lowes.com and www.Home Depot.com. Note the style and type of furnishings, planters, flowers, and other elements. Also, if it's the right time of year, tour your local Target, nurseries, and garden centers for ideas for statuary, furnishings, and planters.

Wonderful Weather

When planning an outdoor room you'll definitely want to take your local weather into consideration. If you live in a cold climate you obviously won't be using the space all year round, or perhaps you will use and enjoy it differently depending on the seasons, so plan accordingly.

Climate matters greatly for the maximum success and enjoyment of your outdoor space. The tiny apartment balcony Steve and I turned into our "urban garden" sitting room, complete with its sweet little fountain, comfy loveseat glider, colorful area rug, and hanging swing, had to be shut down during the snowy midwestern winters, and some of the items had to be stored in the balcony closet. We enjoy our current tiny high-rise terrace year-round because the climate in Southern California is always about 68 degrees. We seldom get rain, and no snow. A friend calls our current bistro-like terrace our "petite paradise in the clouds."

Also regarding climate considerations, we purchased much sturdier, weather-resistant outdoor furnishings for our midwestern balcony than we have for our California terrace, so take *your* climate into consideration carefully as you plan what furnishings to buy. You'll also want to note whether or not your outdoor space is covered. Our California sunshine is bright, so patio cushions fade quickly, but we didn't have that problem in the Midwest.

Organized Outdoor Room

Whether or not you'll use your outdoor terrace, balcony, or patio year-round, you'll want it organized like the rooms we've been creating inside your home. Since you'll want your outdoor space to function as an extension of your current living space, creating the feeling of another room, it's best for your outdoor furnishings to complement your indoor décor.

For example, my personal indoor decorating style has Old World cottage indoor garden ambience, with silk plants, antique botanical pictures on the wall, and a coffee table that's a trellis style. So I made sure the little terrace off my living room has furnishings that blend well with my indoor décor. I chose a pretty wrought iron glass-topped table and chairs with floral cushions, creating a seamless (and organized) decorative look between inside and outside. In the small condo we once owned, we painted a faux brick floor in our living room and had a real brick floor on the adjacent outdoor patio, creating an integrated look between indoors and outdoors that also made the space look bigger.

Begin organizing your outdoor room by assessing the space's current clutter status, with your goal being to get rid of anything that won't contribute to the lovely new space you've envisioned. Toss old newspapers, magazines, rusty lawn tools, and junk. Clean the space well, taking the hose to it if need be, and wash the windows. Once your space is clean and dry, inspect the area carefully and see to any repairs or painting. Make sure your flooring is in safe condition.

After you've made repairs and painted, look at the space once again and decide what feeling or ambience you want to create and what furniture style best suits you. My hubby and I personally love creating terraces that have a romantic outdoor bistro feel by adding gurgling fountains, elegant statues, wrought iron tables, strings of white lights, wicker chairs with floral pillows, and soft silk plants. You might prefer straight-line redwood furniture and planters with real green plants and no flowers. Make it a point to express your own unique taste in your little outdoor dream room, just like you do inside your home.

Getting Organized

Some ideas to consider for outdoor organization and storage:

- If you're planning to host barbecues for friends, hang your grilling utensils on hooks on a nearby fence or wall, or put them in a plastic bin on the bottom shelf of your grill. My hubby once installed a shelf beside his grill that flipped up so he could put the burgers and sauce on the shelf while grilling and flip the shelf down when not in use.

- Make sure you place your grill in a safe area and where it won't blow smoke into your home. And if you live in a condo or apartment, check with the management because sometimes grills are not allowed on balconies and terraces due to fire codes.

- If you want a table and chairs, consider a tiny bistro set like many coffee shops use. Round tables create a cozy feeling and foster intimacy, and you won't be bumping into any square corners. Buy extra folding chairs to store against the wall for when you want to accommodate more than two people. Folding chairs save space.

- Cover your table with a large tablecloth or a charming old quilt and store garden supplies underneath the table in pots or urns.

- Durable opaque plastic lidded storage bins work great for storing hoses, charcoal and lighter fluid, etc. Stack them in a corner and hide them with a decorative metal screen that's painted with Rusto-leum to withstand weather.

- If you have a loveseat or glider, an old wicker trunk makes a nice coffee table and can also store items such as barbecue utensils and supplies.

- Lining the inside of a balcony railing with lattice makes a lovely private garden look, and you can hang gardening tools on hooks on the lattice.

- Use white five-gallon pails with lids to store tools and supplies, and tuck the pails into a corner behind a decorative screen.

- If you have a closet door, over-the-door shoe holder pockets work great for holding garden and barbecue tools.

- For one of our outdoor patios, I bought a used wooden drop-down desk and painted it to match the floral cushions on my chairs. I staged my pots and garden tools artfully on the top, kept potting soil in the drawers, and used the drop-down part of the desk for potting plants. Handy dandy for just a small expense, and it was a conversation piece.

- If you plan to play board games or cards outside on your patio, store them in heavy opaque plastic containers or inside a plastic bench that's waterproof.

- Colorful planters or urns work well for holding garden tools and look attractive too.

- We bought a small portable Rubbermaid shed with doors and shelves that fit into a corner on one of our patios, and we stored extra paint cans and garden tools in it.

- Durable plastic storage benches work great for extra seating if you have room, and you can store items inside.

Lighting Love and Perfect Power

Be sure you have adequate lighting for your outdoor room and also enough power to enjoy all the things you want to in this space. For romantic lighting, I personally love to add tiny white Christmas tree lights to my terrace to create ambience. I wind them around big green ficus trees, and we also draped strings behind our patio lattice for a pretty little glow. Candles add a nice lighting touch, but follow candle safety rules and be careful of wind.

Serene Sounds

A gurgling fountain, wind chimes we found on vacation, and some piped-in music added soothing sounds to our former seaside condo patio. My hubby told me that now you can even buy fake rocks that are stereo speakers! What sounds would you like to have on your patio or terrace?

Organizing for Outdoor Entertaining

I consider entertaining in one's home to be one of life's greatest pleasures. Entertaining can be extra fun to do outside on the patio when the weather is beautiful and your terrace is a lovely outdoor room. I'd like to share with you my ideas for organized and enjoyable outdoor entertaining as well as some examples of special friendship gatherings we've held outdoors.

Again, use the *KISS* principle. There's no need for elaborate preparations when entertaining outdoors. Keep it easy-breezy so you don't have to worry about transporting more food or other stuff than necessary to your outdoor space. But simple doesn't mean it can't be festive, creative, and attractive!

Outdoor Entertaining Ideas from Our "Bechen Bistro"

- I often set up a buffet inside and let guests take their plates to the patio. My hubby and I make sure our guests receive beverage refills, and we remove their plates when they're done so we can continue to visit outdoors and enjoy our time together.

- I like to decorate my little round terrace table with a floral tablecloth, some fresh flowers, china, and silver spoons, and invite just one friend over for a cup of tea and a sweet treat while we sit and chat. Simple, pretty, and a great way to get to know someone better.

- One Fourth of July, I put a red bedsheet over a card table and used a flag motif with red and white flowers to decorate. The couple we invited to join us later said how much they enjoyed the festive summer holiday, and we had a nice conversation while sitting next to the little goldfish pond (left from a former owner) on our small seaside patio.

- My hubby and I set up four card tables end to end on the 16' × 25' patio of our beach condo. We had recently turned the space into a petite garden paradise complete with a stone fountain, white lattice lining the entire space, a mermaid statue, beautiful planters filled with colorful floral plants and trees, and a charming floor made from old bricks. We were longing to celebrate and share it with friends, so we covered the card tables with extra-long rose-motif sheets and the chair backs with matching pillow cases. Next to our rose-patterned china we found in an antique store, we placed vases of pink roses, along with lots of flickering tea lights. At sunset we hosted a dinner party for our church group, and the eight of us had a fabulous time that evening enjoying the ambience of "seaside romance."

- One summer I invited several girlfriends to a Victorian tea party on our backyard patio that was adjacent to my small house and lawn. I set the table in a Victorian setting with lace, silver, and china I had on hand, and I prepared the food inside ahead of time. My guests went through a buffet line in the dining room and then took their own plates outdoors to the patio. They loved it.

- Steve and I once hosted a bridal shower on our backyard patio. Since I was one of the bridesmaids, we had a barbecue for the bride's family the night before the rehearsal dinner. It was a great stress reliever for them to have a casual time eating burgers and having fun as we all sat around our patio table under the colorful umbrella and told funny stories.

Mellow Movies

A former co-worker shared this clever idea for a fun evening on the patio. He said when his kids were little, they set up folding chairs on their small backyard patio one summer evening and showed a movie and served popcorn and soda. The invitation said, *Please Come to Our Cinema Under the Stars.* Now *that's* a fun invitation I'd remember forever!

Never Too Small

Don't think for even a moment that just because you have a tiny terrace or patio you can't entertain outdoors. I'll never forget what a lady once told me while we were visiting on the large patio at a fancy summer soiree given by a mutual friend: "Oh, I never entertain because I live in a tiny condo!" When I asked her where she lived, it was the same condo complex I lived in, with the same 922-square-foot floor plan as mine. As I've already shared with you, we've had some wonderful gatherings, dinners, and fellowship on our 16′ × 25′ patio adjacent to that little condo.

Fond Farewell

I'm really glad we've had this time together sharing how to organize and finesse your little terrace or patio so that you'll be able to really enjoy it every day. I hope you'll take my organizing tips and tidbits and get started *today* in making your space one that you'll absolutely love to share with family and friends. And I also hope you'll retreat to it as a special space for yourself.

Resources for Small Terraces and Patios

Bistro Tables
www.BallardDesigns.com
www.HomeDecorators.com
www.Target.com

Garden Statuary
www.HomeDepot.com
www.Lowes.com
www.Target.com

Lattice to Fence In a Patio or Terrace
www.HomeDepot.com
www.Lowes.com

Outdoor Furniture
www.BallardDesigns.com
www.HomeDepot.com
www.Lowes.com
www.Target.com

Outdoor Lighting
www.HomeDepot.com
www.Lowes.com

Outdoor Stereo Speakers
www.AllOutdoorSpeaker.com
www.OutdoorSpeakerDepot.com

Plastic Lidded Storage Bins
www.ContainerStore.com
www.Target.com
www.WalMart.com

Rubbermaid Outdoor Storage Closets
www.HomeDepot.com
www.Lowes.com
www.Rubbermaid.com

YOUR SMALL SPACE NOTES

_____

_____

_____

_____

_____

_____

_____

_____

_____

_____

_____

_____

_____

_____

_____

_____

_____

_____

_____

Oh Storage, Where Art Thou?

Here's a sad storage tale: My hubby came home from the grocery store the other day (ironically, while I was writing a book on home organizing!) and told me that a lady in front of him at the checkout told the cashier that she was so frustrated because her husband was paying $900 a month for a storage unit. "What good does it do to downsize our home," she said, "if you're just going to pay big bucks to store so much stuff in a storage unit?"

Amen! In some parts of the United States he could've rented a whole apartment for that amount! And if you add up the rent for just one year, he's spending $10,800 a year on storing "stuff." Multiply that times five years and it's $54,000! Wouldn't that be a nice sum for your child's college fund, your IRA, or world travel?

I strongly believe you should only rent storage units for two reasons:

1. To store archived business and personal paper documents that you absolutely must keep.
2. To temporarily store possessions when you're in the process of relocating.

Other than that, if you are careful not to succumb to "possession obsession," and if you declutter your home and home office regularly, you won't *need* a storage unit. Save the money and take a cruise is my motto!

Ah well, you say, that's all fine and good *in a perfect world*. But alas, in most people's small space *real world*, there's at least one storage closet, outside shed, rented storage unit, or garage to be found. So I'll help you out a bit here with some organizing tips for those spaces.

Storage Rental Unit

Renting an off-site storage unit is sometimes necessary for archiving personal and business files, or for temporarily housing household goods when you're in the transition of moving from one home to another. When we were selling our condo, for instance, we professionally staged it, so we rented a storage unit temporarily until our home sold. Key word: *temporarily*. Again, please be hypervigilant about renting storage units and don't spend your hard-earned money on them unless absolutely necessary.

Archive File Storage M.O.

When archiving business papers and tax records in a storage unit, be sure to use plastic lidded bins with labeled hanging file folders inside. Don't use cardboard banker's boxes for your files, because they get dirty and don't wipe off easily, they crush when stacked, and they are also subject to moisture. Plastic bins will keep your papers dry and are sturdier, making them better able to hold the weight of the files when you stack the bins.

Label It, Mabel!

Be sure to label the front of each bin with your label maker and stack the bins in alphabetical order and also by year if appropriate (taxes, for instance). Stack the bins around the perimeter of the storage unit. Remember that because of the weight of the files, you can only stack them about three high or the lids may crack and cave in.

List, Lighting, and Keys

After you've arranged all your bins, you'll want to write or type up a list/index of all the files. Keep one copy of the list in the unit and one copy at home so that if you wonder what you did with "File X," you can easily find it. Remember to update the list if you add or subtract a box from the unit. Also, buy a portable battery-operated camping lantern for lighting since most storage facilities don't have lighting inside individual units. And be sure to get two keys to your unit so that more than one family member has access to the files. It's also a good idea to leave a key with your estate planning attorney. And of course, once a year go through your archive files and shred what no longer needs to be kept.

Relocation Storage Unit

Just a word about renting a storage unit temporarily while you're relocating. Be sure to think through how you will stack your household items in your unit and don't just shove them all in there. Put least important or least used items in the back and items used most often in the front. Place items around the perimeter of the room so you can stand in the middle of the unit and easily find what you need.

Indoor Storage Closet

My hubby and I live in a 1,200-square-foot high-rise apartment with no garage storage, no rented storage unit, and just one 6′ × 8′ walk-in closet in which to store our archive paper files, extra office supplies, tools, and miscellaneous household and travel items. I want to share with you how we have arranged our closet to give you some ideas.

Everything is stacked neatly around the perimeter of the closet so we can stand in the center of the walk-in closet and see at a glance what's in there. Labeled bins of archived business and tax files are stacked along one whole wall. On the adjacent wall are white wire shelves with labeled plastic bins that hold Steve's few tools. We store our ladder between two of the shelves; our vacuum and carpet cleaners stand in front of the shelves and are moved when we need to get a tool. On the third wall suitcases are stacked along with our memorabilia/treasure bins (one each), computer carrying cases, first aid box, and emergency evacuation bins containing all our important papers and computer disks so we can just grab and go should an earthquake strike. We also have a few pieces of art that are covered with brown paper and labeled. That's it! We go through our storage closet once a year and make sure our files are cleared out and current.

Outdoor Storage Sheds

If you are using an outdoor storage shed, please realize that storage sheds are subject to moisture from rain and snow that could cause mold or mildew. So it's better to store papers in indoor closets or interior rented storage units that are climate controlled. Also, outdoor sheds are vulnerable to rodents and thieves, so be sure to adequately lock your shed for security.

Gorgeous Garage

Is your garage gorgeous or gluttonous? I consulted a "garage expert" (a.k.a. my hubby) and asked him how he organized our small garages in the past. Here's what he said:

> First and foremost, your car should fit in the garage. Then all you really need is a moveable workbench, a rolling tool chest, a pegboard to mount large tools on the wall, large ceiling hooks to hang bikes and skis, and sports racks you purchase for golf clubs and other sports equipment can stand along the walls. The less stuff, the better.

He also put an old piece of carpet in the middle of our garage to catch any leaks from underneath our car.

Savvy Storage

I'd like to wrap things up for you in this last chapter by taking you on a special room-by-room tour of small homes, condos, and apartments I've visited over the years as an organizer, writer, and friend. So come on, let's go on one last small space home tour together and see some creative storage ideas!

Fab Foyer

A good friend of mine has the most organized, personalized, and welcoming foyer I've ever seen. She used her grandmother's antique cabinet as the focal point, storing her kids' mittens and caps in the drawers. She labeled an in-box basket for each child's school papers and keeps them on a cabinet shelf. Shoes are kept in rectangular cake pans underneath the cabinet to keep the floor clean. Antique wall hooks that belonged to her grandfather hold the family's coats. She covered bulletin boards with vintage-looking wrapping paper and hung keys and notes for her kids on there. Lovely!

Kitchen Kudos

An acquaintance of mine has the most adorable and functional small space kitchen. She hired a builder who specializes in building boat cabinetry to design her kitchen cabinets. A row of glass-front cabinets on top displays her colorful dishes, and a door that flips up and then recesses into the wall covers the front of the microwave. Little nooks and crannies were designed to hold plates and utensils, and drawers pull out to easily store pans. She also has a built-in spice rack above her range.

One client of mine used soft-sided round zippered plastic cases to store her china in her kitchen. She displayed her rice, beans, and cereals in clear glass gallon jars on her counter, which added a homey touch to her kitchen. Mugs hung on hooks under her cabinets, and a round spinner with hooks for coffee cups hung inside one cabinet.

A single guy I know has a charming small urban kitchen. He loves to cook and has a pot rack mounted from the ceiling for ambience. He uses antique crocks, pitchers, and old trophy cups he's collected for storing his cooking utensils on the counters. An over-the-door shoe holder hangs on the back of his small pantry door for storing sauce mixes, teabags, gum, and other small items. Baskets on the counters hold his folded placemats and dish towels.

Bathroom Bliss

A former client of mine had a tiny but oh-so-cute bathroom. Decorated to match her master bedroom, the bathroom was stocked with baskets of tiny hotel soaps and shampoos she'd collected during her world travels. She rolled up fluffy towels and stored them in a big wicker basket. She hung a pretty decorative hook on the back of the door for her robe and added an over-the-toilet cabinet to store her shampoo and other toiletries.

I visited a friend once who had a bathroom that you could barely turn around in! But it was cute, and she had some clever storage. She purchased a very slim tiered wire cart on casters and put it between her tub and the toilet for folded towels. She found a tall antique shelf at an auction and hung it over her toilet for more towels and toiletries. She replaced the old medicine cabinet with a much larger mirrored one to add even more toiletry storage, and she sewed a fabric skirt for around the pedestal sink and stored toilet paper behind the skirt.

Living Room Love

A small studio apartment I visited had savvy storage. A twin bed with a trundle bed underneath also served as a sofa. The kitchen table was on hinges on the wall and was pulled up for meals. The coffee table was a wicker trunk that was used to store extra blankets.

In another small living room I toured, the owners made great use of storage with floor-to-ceiling bookcases on either side of the fireplace. Their coffee table was an ottoman with a hinged top so they could store games inside, and their game table in the corner was a round space-saving antique gateleg table.

Master Bedroom Haven

A small but beautiful master bedroom I visited had bookcases built all across the wall that the bed stood against. The shelves stored books and items collected from the homeowners' travels. They had a bench at the foot of their bed to store extra blankets, and an antique TV cabinet housed their DVD player and movies. Plastic under-the-bed lidded storage bins held out-of-season clothes. The walk-in closet was custom-designed to accommodate both the husband's and wife's unique needs. It featured cubbies for shoes, double-hung rods, and shallow pullout trays for jewelry.

Glowing Guest Room

A friend of mine has a beautiful little guest room. It has a white wicker headboard and wicker nightstands that hold DVDs and toys, a colorful quilt she made herself, and big fluffy pillows. A toy box holds dolls, there's a small play table, and shelves in the closet house books and games. What fun!

So Long, Storage!

Remember that one blessing of living in a small space is that it acts as a container of sorts—containing you from collecting too many possessions. So count your blessings for that, and keep your storage needs to a minimum by following the tips and tricks in this chapter.

Resources for Small Space Storage

Document Shredding
www.Goodwill.org

File Bins with Lids for Paper File Archival
www.ContainerStore.com
www.OfficeDepot.com
www.Target.com

Outdoor Storage Sheds and Bins
www.HomeDepot.com
www.Lowes.com
www.Rubbermaid.com

Pegboard for Garages
www.HomeDepot.com
www.Lowes.com

Portable Camping Lanterns
www.HomeDepot.com
www.Lowes.com
www.Target.com

Portable Garage Workbenches and Tool Boxes
www.HomeDepot.com
www.Lowes.com
www.Target.com

Round Zippered Cases for China Dishes
www.ContainerStore.com
www.TheFind.com

Sports Equipment Storage
www.ContainerStore.com
www.OrganizeIt.com
www.Target.com

YOUR SMALL SPACE NOTES

Small Space Farewell

My small space friend, we've come a long way together in the pages of this book, touring virtually every nook and cranny of many types of small space homes, including my own and those of my clients, friends, and acquaintants. We've peered into and rearranged kitchen cupboards, sorted through storage closets, and learned how to transform a plain tiny terrace into a petite garden paradise.

It's been my great pleasure to share my organizing ideas, tips, and strategies with you. I hope I've motivated and inspired you to create a home for yourself that's organized enough for comfort and personalized enough so it feels oh-so-you. I hope you laughed a bit throughout this book, too, because organizing your home can, and should, be *fun*.

I now wish you a fond small space farewell, and I leave you with these parting thoughts.

When I recently asked someone to share his most vivid memory of growing up in a small apartment in the midst of a huge bustling city, he immediately replied, "I felt safe there." Not necessarily something we'd think a person would say about living in the heart of the inner city, but his cozy apartment, devoted father, and the neighbors in his building and neighborhood who became his friends *made it so.*

Indeed, small space homes snugly house our happy memories, but perhaps more importantly, when life feels hard, they cradle us in the shelter of their comforting arms. Like a loving, long-time mate we can tell our heartfelt secrets to, they are our safe cocoon, our intimate haven.

My sincere wish for you, my friend, is that you will embrace the fullness of your small space lifestyle, with all the blessings and freedoms it offers. And remember what William Morris once said: "Have nothing in your house that you do not know to be useful, or believe to be beautiful."

Small Space Lifestyle Conversations

Jonathan, New York City, Apartment, 1,200 Square Feet

Q: *How large was your small space and how many people lived there?*

A: I grew up in a 1,200-square-foot apartment on the fourteenth floor where I lived with my father.

Q: *Did you have a terrace or patio?*

A: No.

Q: *Since you had a small indoor space, did you ever feel cramped as an active boy?*

A: At one point I had a friend who lived in the suburbs, and I asked my father if we could get a "real house" and a dog. But most of the time I was content with my life in an urban apartment and had great fun in our neighborhood. And I had my little critters: hamsters, gerbils, and turtles.

Q: *Since you didn't have a yard to play in, did you enjoy parks, museums, or other outdoor activities?*

A: There were playgrounds near us, and we had great fun playing outdoor basketball and Little League. I went to museums during school field trips. And my father sent me to summer camp in the country, and then when it was over we would take a father/son trip together, so I had the best of the city and the country.

Q: *Did you have an eat-in kitchen or a dining room?*

A: We had both, but since it was just the two of us, we usually ate in the kitchen at a small table, and we went to visit friends or relatives on holidays rather than entertain them at our apartment.

Q: *What was your bedroom like and how did you organize it?*

A: I had my own bedroom with a big bathroom I really liked. Sometimes just for fun I'd rearrange my furniture, and I personalized my room by posting things I collected on a bulletin board. And of course [he laughs], I hung a Farah Fawcett poster on the wall, like all boys did back then! It was a big deal when my dad let me pick out my own window blinds and carpeting for my room.

Q: *What did you like most about living in a small apartment in New York City?*

A: I felt safe. It was my world; I made friends in my building, including one sweet older lady who lived to be about one hundred! I loved getting to know people in my neighborhood and having the ever-present vibe of bustling New York City around me.

Q: *Now that you live in a single-family home in Arizona, what do you miss about your urban apartment lifestyle in New York City?*

A: I miss things like being able to walk right out of our apartment and smell pizza coming from the little neighborhood pizzeria, Central Park, the egg creams at the newsstand across the street, rye bread at the local deli, and making Christmas tree forts.

Q: *Would you ever like to live in a small urban apartment again?*

A: My family and I are happy now in Arizona, but I'd also love to buy an apartment in Manhattan and share the urban experience with them. I've taken my young son back to visit my old neighborhood, and we had great fun. I wouldn't trade what I experienced growing up in the Big Apple for anything because it taught me to be tolerant and aware of many different kinds of people. There was always excitement. For me, it gave me an education that my college years could never teach me. Living there was like getting "a degree in life."

Elizabeth and Jerry, Small Midwest Town, Two-Story House, 1,300 Square Feet

Q: *When did you rent your small two-story house?*

A: When we were first married; we've lived here twenty-five years now!

Q: *Why did you rent for such a long time, rather than buy a home?*

A: This was what we could afford at the time, and we've liked the neighborhood so much, the school, and the fact that the landlord did all the maintenance kept us content with renting versus buying another home.

Q: *Have you done anything to fix the house up?*

A: We take care of minor household repairs but the landlord does the big stuff, which suits us fine as we aren't handyman type people. He's done some nice remodeling and let us have input.

Q: *What's your favorite thing about the house?*

A: I love the breakfast nook in the kitchen with the built-in benches. I have a friend who comes every Friday before work to chat over tea and I make us breakfast. We've been doing that for about twenty years! Our husbands think we're crazy to get up that early, but we have fun keeping up on each other's lives.

Q: *What do you like least about the house?*

A: We have virtually no yard, so our kids haven't had much place to play. Luckily there's a park down the street, so that's been their playground.

Q: *Do you have a garage?*

A: No. When these homes in this neighborhood were built, most had no garages so we park our cars on the street. It's a challenge in the winter sometimes, but you get used to it.

Q: *If you don't have a garage, where do you store your "stuff"?*

A: We have a small basement. That works fine because we try not to accumulate a lot of stuff so we don't need that much storage.

Q: *What's your favorite memory about living in this house?*

A: It's both a good memory and a sad one, actually. The good part is we redecorated our master bedroom this year with the help of my friend in New York who gave us ideas because he's an interior designer. The sad news is we did it as a haven for my husband who was diagnosed with a difficult disease. I wish we had done it sooner.

Q: *I'm sorry to hear about your husband. How has his illness changed how you live in your home?*

A: We spend more quiet nights together just watching TV and snuggling together. It's brought us closer, and we realize how precious our life together is. We don't need a big house; we have each other to love, and that's enough for us.

Q: *Do you have extended family that come to visit, and if so, where do they sleep?*

A: The house has three tiny bedrooms that our family uses and a little alcove attic room that we've turned into a cute guest room. Our friends and family seem to be content staying there because it's kind of a fun hideaway that we decorated with antiques and a cozy colorful quilt. We like having a place for overnight guests; I wouldn't feel comfortable sending people to a hotel.

Q: *You've lived here for so long, do you think you'll ever move from this place?*

A: Although we love it here, we do realize that life has its seasons. With our kids almost grown, there will come a day when a small condo is more suitable for us.

Jane, Midsize College Town, East Coast, Bungalow, 1,100 Square Feet

Q: *How large was your small space, and how many people lived there?*

A: We lived in an 1,100-square-foot bungalow-style house. There were four of us in the family at the time.

Q: *Did you ever feel cramped there?*

A: No. We had a front porch and were often outside having fun in the neighborhood with other kids and our dog, so I don't remember our home feeling crowded at all.

Q: *Did you have a yard?*

A: Yes, we had a small front yard and a large, fenced-in backyard where we played and had a tree house. There was a little stream running through our backyard and my father built a bridge to go over it.

Q: *Did you have an eat-in kitchen or a dining room?*

A: We had both. We used the kitchen table for breakfast and the dining room for lunch and dinner.

Q: *Did you ever have friends to dinner?*

A: Oh yes! We loved having barbecues in our backyard and inviting our friends and neighbors. On the Fourth of

July we always had a big party. The kids ran through the sprinklers to stay cool. We had such fun! In the winter we had friends over for chili. It was nothing fancy, but we loved the fellowship of being together and we'd hold hands around our dining table and pray before the meal.

Q: *What was your bedroom like and how did you organize and decorate it?*

A: It was right off of our living room and I remember it being very cozy and we had wool flowered carpeting, believe it or not. I was just five years old when we lived there, and I remember my mom teaching me to make my bed every day, and we picked out wallpaper and a closet organizer together, as well as my twin bed head-board.

Q: *What did you like most about living in a small home in a small college town?*

A: It was a simple, safe life. I walked a couple of blocks to school all by myself even though I was only five. I made friends in the neighborhood, and I loved going to church school. Everything centered around family, school, and church. There was community.

Q: *Now that you live in an urban loft condo in San Francisco, do you ever long for that simple bungalow lifestyle?*

A: I'm happy with my life now, which is simple in a different way because I don't have home maintenance because we have an on-call maintenance crew. But yes, sometimes I long for the small- town "front porch friendly" lifestyle where neighbors still sit and chat with each other over an iced tea. A bungalow seems a million miles away from my lifestyle today, but I know it still exists.

Q: *What was your favorite thing about living in a bungalow?*
A: The front porch and chatting with neighbors. Definitely.

Q: *If you had to choose between raising your own children in an urban loft or in a small-town bungalow, which would you choose?*
A: Both have their merits, really. Obviously an urban loft doesn't have a big yard for kids to play, but we have two Olympic-size swimming pools and a miniature golf area, and we can walk to restaurants. Raising my kids in a bungalow in a small town would be idyllic in some ways, yet there are not usually many cultural events to expose them to there, which I think is important. So it's a toss-up really, I'd say.

Marilyn, San Francisco, Studio Condominium, 500 Square Feet

Q: *Why did you choose to buy a small studio condo?*
A: My husband passed away last year, and I decided to sell our large home and buy a studio with a sneak peek view of the Golden Gate Bridge so I would have the time and money to travel, rather than maintain a large house and yard.

Q: *Are you happy with your decision after living in a large home for more than forty years?*
A: Absolutely! I feel free as a bird!

Q: *What do you like most about your small space?*

A: I hired an interior designer to help me decorate the space and to maximize the storage. I am very pleased with how it turned out.

Q: *What did the designer do that was so helpful to you?*

A: She really helped me translate my unique personality and taste in décor into the space so it feels very "autobiographical" for who I am as a person in my current life. I have a wall painted a gorgeous lavender with accent chairs near it that we had recovered in a deep purple and two other chairs that are bright yellow. It's a *wow* combo!

Q: *What do you like most about your storage in your small space?*

A: The designer helped me choose a home office armoire that fits perfectly in my kitchen. When closed up, it looks like a beautiful wooden hutch. When down, it's a very convenient way for me to stay connected virtually with friends from around the world with my laptop computer and phone. The designer also suggested floor-to-ceiling bookcases along the wall in the living room, and I love the look *and* the storage for my books and objects my husband and I collected during our forty years of travel.

Q: *What do you like least about living in your small space?*

A: Sometimes I miss not having a garden anymore, but I put several colorful planters and a small bistro table out on my terrace and that pretty much took care of missing my garden! It's a lot less upkeep and a whole lot more fun!

Q: *Since you have no bedroom, where is your bed?*

A: I chose a twin bed with a pull-out trundle for when my granddaughter comes to visit, and the designer had custom pillows made so it doubles as my sofa.

Q: *Since you only live in 500 square feet, do you ever have friends over and entertain?*

A: Absolutely! I have a round glass dining table, which makes the space look larger than if I had a solid table, and I decorated the table and had a stand-up fondue party for fifteen people. And last holiday I set up four card tables end to end in the living room, put a long tablecloth and a beautiful centerpiece on them, and had a sit-down dinner for eight that we served from my kitchen. I set up little dessert trays on the terrace bistro table and we had a fabulous feast! I'm not about to let living in a tiny space stop me from entertaining friends; you just have to go about it differently and make it an elegantly intimate experience. Soft candlelight is good!

Q: *Would you buy the same studio condo again?*

A: Yes! I'm seventy-five years old and love the view and my simplified lifestyle so much that they're going to have to carry me out of here because I'm never moving again!

Home Office Equipment and Supplies List

Desk Area

Comfortable desk with drawers

Comfortable desk chair

Office armoire

Attractive slipcover for desk chair

All-in-one machine (or separate machines)

Computer and printer

Fax machine

Phone

Cell phone

Drawer trays to divide and hold supplies in desk (silverware trays work great)

Paper clips

Binder clips

Highlighters (yellow are best as they do not show through on photocopies)

Post-it flags to mark pages in books or on photocopies

Scotch tape

Carton cutter

Post-it notes in several sizes and colors

Pencil sharpener

Rubber bands

Letter divider to hold envelopes, Post-it notes, etc.

Mugs to hold pens, letter opener, etc.

Wall calendar

Task lighting

Stapler

Staples

Pens (Uni-ball brand roller ball pens are great and come in several colors)

Scissors

Paintbrush to dust desk and computer keys

Index cards for capturing ideas and taking notes

Pencils

Phone message pad

Business card holder

Business cards

Notecards with your logo to write thank-you notes

Legal size mailing envelopes

Letterhead or stationery

Small spiral notebooks for notes

Notepads

Glue stick

Liquid Paper correction fluid

Postage stamps and holder

Paperweight

Calculator

Bold permanent marker pen

Planner calendar with address book (either paper or electronic—whatever works for you)

Caddy to hold hanging file folders

Manila file folders

Manila file pockets

Green hanging files

Green hanging files—box bottom

Clear label holders for green hanging files

Bookcases

Three-ring binders with clear pocket on front (1″, 2″, 3″ sizes in white)

Handheld label maker for binder labels

Three-hole punch

Bookends

Photo boxes (hold a lot of miscellaneous supplies and can be labeled by topic)

Wicker baskets (hold supplies nicely)

Magazine holders

Files

Two-drawer cabinets are low and can be put side-by-side like a credenza and the top used to sort papers etc.

Four-drawer cabinets take up less space and can be placed side-by-side

Plastic file bins to hold hanging files are portable and can be moved around while you work

Other

Wall clock

Paper shredder

Shelf or table for all-in-one copier/printer

Overhead lighting

Task lighting

Air purifier

Doorstop

CD player

Phone directories

Thesaurus

Dictionary

Grammar book

Resources for Small Space Living

Small Space Books

Abdelnour, Christine Brun. *Small Space Living.* Atglen, PA: Schiffer Publishing, 2009.

Banar. *Small Space Survival Guide: Storage and Decorating Tips and Tricks.* Little Rock, AR: Leisure Arts, Inc., 2009.

Culbertson, Judi, and Marj Decker. *Scaling Down: Living Large in a Smaller Space.* Emmaus, PA: Rodale Press, 2005.

Gillingham-Ryan, Maxwell. *Apartment Therapy's Big Book of Small, Cool Spaces.* New York: Clarkson Potter, 2010.

Susanka, Sarah. *The Not So Big House: A Blueprint for the Way We Really Live.* Expanded edition. Newtown, CT: Taunton Press, 2008.

Tanqueray, Rebecca. *Small Spaces: Making the Most of the Space You Have.* Photographs by Chris Everard. New York: Ryland, Peters & Small, 2003.

Ward, Lauri. *Downsizing Your Home with Style: Living Well in a Smaller Space.* New York: HarperCollins, 2007.

Wilhide, Elizabeth. *Small Spaces: Maximizing Limited Spaces for Living.* The Small Book of Home Ideas Series. London: Jacqui Small, 2008.

Small Space Websites and Blogs

www.ApartmentTherapy.com

www.LovingLivingSmall.blogspot.com

www.SarahSusanka.com

www.SmallPlaceStyle.blogspot.com

www.TumbleWeedHouses.com

Home Organizing Resources

Books

Barnes, Emilie. *Emilie's Creative Home Organizer.* Eugene, OR: Harvest House, 2005.

Felton, Sandra. *Living Organized: Proven Steps for a Clutter-Free and Beautiful Home.* Grand Rapids: Revell, 2004.

Kosann, Monica Rich. *Living With What You Love: Decorating With Family Photos, Cherished Heirlooms, and Collectibles.* New York: Clarkson Potter, 2010.

Ramsland, Marcia. *Simplify Your Space: Create Order and Reduce Stress.* Nashville: Thomas Nelson, 2007.

Smallin, Donna. *Unclutter Your Home: 7 Simple Steps, 700 Tips & Ideas.* Pownal, VT: Storey Publishing, 1999.

Moving/Relocation Associations

American Society of Estate Liquidators
    www.ASELonline.com

National Association of Homebuilders
    www.NAHB.org

National Association of Professional Organizers
    www.NAPO.net

National Association of Senior Move Managers
   www.NASMM.org
Unpacking Services
   www.3DaysOrLess.com

Moving/Relocation Books and E-Books

Bechen, Kathryn. *Moving with Ease: The Eight Week Plan for an Organized and Stress Free Move Whether You Hire a Mover or Do It Yourself.* www.KathrynBechenInk.com. 2006. PDF e-book.

Poage, Martha. *The Moving Survival Guide: All You Need to Know to Make Your Move Go Smoothly.* Guilford, CT: Globe Pequot Press, 2004.

Charitable Donations

www.Goodwill.org
www.SalvationArmyUSA.org
Your local library
Your local church

Decluttering/Hauling

1-800-GOT JUNK

Document Shredding

Goodwill Industries
   www.Goodwill.org

Furniture Layout Templates

www.DecoratorTrainingInstitute.com

Organizing Products and Supplies (My Favorites)

www.BallardDesigns.com

www.BedBathandBeyond.com

www.CalClosets.com

www.ClosetsbyDesign.com

www.ContainerStore.com

www.CreativeMemories.com

www.EasyClosets.com

www.Elfa.com

www.ExposuresOnline.com

www.GetOrganizedNow.com

www.HoldEverything.com

www.HomeDecorators.com

www.HomeGoods.com

www.Ikea.com

www.KMart.com

www.Levenger.com

www.LillianVernon.com

www.OfficeDepot.com

www.OnlineOrganizing.com

www.Organize.com

www.Organize-It.com

www.OrganizedAtoZ.com

www.ShopGetOrganized.com

www.StacksandStacks.com

www.Target.com

www.WalMart.com

www.WestElm.com

Professional Organizers

National Association of Professional Organizers

www.NAPO.net

Kathryn Bechen is an award-winning professional lifestyle writer whose articles have appeared in popular national newsstand magazines including *Small Room Decorating*, *Cottage Style*, *Cottages & Cabins*, *Country Almanac*, *Country Victorian*, and in regional magazines such as *San Diego Style Weddings* and *Nebraska Wedding Day*. Her work has also been published in numerous print newspapers and online.

Quoted repeatedly in the media for her organizing and decorating expertise, Kathryn holds a BA degree in English and education and a certificate in interior decorating. The lifestyle companies she founded—Organized With Ease, Kathryn Bechen Designs, and KathrynBechen.com—have served clients worldwide.

Kathryn has organized and decorated thirteen personal small space residences together with her husband, Steve, during their thirty-plus years of marriage, and they currently reside in their favorite small space ever: a 1,200-square-foot high-rise apartment in beautiful San Diego, California.

To sign up for Kathryn's free lifestyle e-newsletter and to learn more about her books, e-books, blog, and media interviews, please visit her website at www.KathrynBechen .com. You can also locate Kathryn on Facebook, Twitter, and LinkedIn.

**For More Resources to
Simplify and Enhance
Your Home and Life**

Connect with

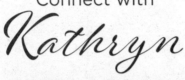

Kathryn

Kathrynbechen.com